Lunch with Lady Eaton

Lunch with Lady Eaton

INSIDE THE DINING ROOMS OF A NATION

Text and Photographic Research by Carol Anderson

Recipes by Katharine Mallinson

ECW Press

for Joan Caruso

Published by ECW PRESS
2120 Queen Street East, Suite 200, Toronto, Ontario, Canada M4E 1E2

NATIONAL LIBRARY OF CANADA CATALOGUING IN PUBLICATION

Anderson, Carol
Lunch with Lady Eaton : inside the dining rooms of a nation /
Carol Anderson and Katharine Mallinson.

Includes index.
ISBN 1-55022-650-9

1. Eaton, Flora McCrea, 1880-1970 — Contributions in entertaining.
2. Entertaining — Canada. 3. Dinners and dining — Canada. I. Mallinson, Katharine II. Title.

TX910.5.E28A53 2004 647.95'092 C2004-900106-X

Editor: Joy Gugeler
Cover, Text Design, and Layout: Tania Craan
Printing: Book Art

This book is set in Garamond.

5 4 3 2

The publication of *Lunch with Lady Eaton* has been generously supported by the Canada Council, the Ontario Arts Council, and the Government of Canada through the Book Publishing Industry Development Program. Canada

DISTRIBUTION
CANADA: Jaguar Book Group, 100 Armstrong Avenue, Georgetown, ON, L7G 5S4

PRINTED IN HONG KONG

ECW PRESS
ecwpress.com

Contents

Prologue

Timothy Eaton was "shopkeeper to a nation" for more than a century, establishing stores in virtually all major Canadian cities, as well as an enormous mail-order business, at a time when a Canadian department store had little international competition. Throughout the 1900s, Eaton's occupied a key role in the country's economic and political culture, celebrated as a trusted family-owned business capable of bringing Canadian and international goods into Canadian homes.

In Eaton's nascence in the late 19th century, much of the Canadian population lived on farms and in small towns. Timothy Eaton's marketing genius lay in recognizing and accommodating the growing buying power of this middle class, catering to buyers in rural areas by offering Eaton's catalogue and delivery services that allowed them access to everything from plows to groceries, from sleighs to jams and jellies. The catalogue also endured, through long Canadian winters, as popular escapist reading.

Eaton's offered convenience, expedience, vision and attention to detail as it attracted women shoppers in urban centres by enticing them into the store with services, affordable goods and consideration for their needs. These trademarks were especially visible in Eaton's fine restaurants, which provided good food in comfortable surroundings and offered places where friends met for lunch and grandmothers spoiled their grandchildren on holidays and birthdays. They were an elegant place to lunch, a Canadian innovation, a haven and a place to celebrate.

The Eaton family owned two dairy farms in Georgetown and in Islington, areas now a part of the Greater Toronto Area sprawl, but which a century ago were idyllic countryside, far beyond the outskirts of the city. Products from the family farms and dairy provided prepared foods for sale in the country's stores, at grand bakery counters and soda fountains, and in the company's restaurants.

Winnipeg's Grill Room opened in 1905, the Georgian Room debuted in Toronto's flagship Queen Street store in 1924; Hamilton's Pansy Room in 1927 (which became the Green Room soon after its opening); College Street's Round Room in 1930; Le 9e, the ninth floor restaurant in the Montreal store, in 1931. The Marine Room in

Vancouver joined the list in 1949; Yorkdale's Vista Room in 1964; and the Mayfair Room in London in 1970. A trio of "Sir John's" restaurants, named after Lady Eaton's husband, operated briefly in Kitchener, at Winnipeg's Polo Park and in the men's fashions department of the Toronto Eaton Centre later in the century.

Flora McCrea Eaton, wife of the store's second president, John Craig Eaton, was at the helm of the flagship restaurants noted above. A philanthropist, advocate of arts and culture, socialite, singer, world traveller and mother of six, she joined Eaton's Board of Directors in 1921 and influenced decisions there until her retirement in 1943. Timothy Eaton recognized in his daughter-in-law a keen business sense, drive and a vision that informed every aspect of the business.

Lady Eaton was a notable figure in Canadian life for almost seven decades, a woman who took her role as a public figure seriously. Through her determination and her efforts in many areas, from cuisine to the theatre, Lady Eaton extended the philanthropic reach of the Eaton family until the family's status could be said to be as close to royalty as has existed in Canada. At the time of her death, the Prime Minister of the day, Pierre Elliot Trudeau, eulogized her as "a moving force" and marked her passing as "the end of an era — an era of overwhelming changes and growth — in which Lady Eaton always took a lively interest" (*Peterborough Examiner*, July 10, 1970).

In this era, Eaton's provides us with a nostalgic view of Canadian life at a time when products were linked to the seasons and the land,

and to a pace and gentility that has disappeared forever. Recipes, ingredients and notes on food preparation provide a fascinating snapshot of the time. *Lunch with Lady Eaton* includes a selection of these recipes, tested and measured for today's homes, from the kitchens of the Georgian Room, the Round Room, Le 9e, Winnipeg's Grill Room and the stores' bakery counters. The restaurants prided themselves on offering a national cuisine — their menus and recipes reflected a consensus: this was what Canadians deemed good to eat. Lady Eaton and her kitchen staff pioneered training for commercial dietitians in Canada (a model later borrowed by the military in World War II) and planned elegant menus requiring, by today's standards, relatively few ingredients. As produce is now available anytime from anywhere, local and seasonal produce is no longer a consideration in cooking, and inventiveness necessitated by scarcity has largely disappeared. The recipes in *Lunch with Lady Eaton* make it possible to enjoy historic, well-loved treats. They offer, along with the sweets and savouries, a taste of a vanished Canada.

Lunch with Lady Eaton

Goods Satisfactory or Money Refunded

As a boy, Timothy Eaton had been apprenticed to a storekeeper in Ireland. He was harshly treated and slept under the store's counter, an experience that steeled his resolve to treat his own employees with consideration. After emigrating from Ireland in 1854, he pursued a number of early business ventures, including operating a bakery and a small dry-goods business. His first store was in Kirkton, Ontario, started in 1856 in partnership with his brother James, who had emigrated earlier. Sensing new opportunities, Timothy moved on to St. Mary's, Ontario, in 1860 and by May of the next year, he was advertising a new store on the town's Queen Street, offering a large variety of dry goods, boots, shoes, kitchenware, hardware, farming tools, crockery and patent medicines. In 1868 he made the leap to

Private dining room adjacent to Toronto Grill Room, May 24, 1911

Toronto and with capital of $6,500 leased a storefront property at 178 Yonge Street, at the corner of Yonge and Queen Streets. Eaton opened the doors of T. Eaton & Co. here on December 8, 1869, with four employees.

Timothy Eaton was a visionary businessman. As working people made it clear they wanted a wide range of goods under one roof at affordable prices to fit their tight budgets, he altered his retail policies to provide an enormous variety and volume of products at reasonable and fixed prices. Cash sales and firm prices were highly unusual at the time; bartering and prices that changed during the course of a transaction were then the norm in merchandising. Timothy Eaton's idea of "cash and one price only" was very attractive to Eaton's clientele, who now knew exactly how much they could afford and where to find it.

A highly principled man and a devoted churchgoer, Timothy Eaton forbade the sale of alcohol, playing cards and tobacco on Eaton's premises. The company's restaurants served no alcohol until the 1970s. Eaton prided himself on honesty, and kept a list of words he considered misleading or excessive that were never to be used in advertisements. For many years, Timothy Eaton wrote the advertisements and slogans himself. The store's longstanding promise, "Goods satisfactory or money refunded," was a resolute assurance of quality and service.

"Get your lunch" trade card, 1900

Eaton's business grew steadily and by 1882 Timothy Eaton took over the Page Block, three adjoining stores north of Queen Street at 190–196 Yonge Street. These stores were demolished and replaced with one building with large plate-glass display windows facing the street. The new store had 35 departments in its three storeys, including women's fashions, footwear, millinery, linens, lace, carpets, leather goods, china and dry goods.

Timothy Eaton's business acumen allowed him to capitalize on the rising buying power of middle-class women. He wooed them into his original Queen Street store with goods from all over the world, with conveniences and with special consideration for their preferences. Buses met shoppers, whether they were arriving in the city by train or by boat, to carry them free of charge to the Queen Street store. There they were welcomed by doormen who assisted them with

Soda fountain, main floor, Queen Street store (James Street section), 1905. The countertop is marbled zinc.

their packages while floorwalkers helped them on and off the elevators. An area with comfortable change rooms and full-length mirrors was provided for fittings. In the Ladies Gallery and Waiting Room, women could rest, meet a friend, even have a bath. Their children could be cared for by nurses while they made their purchases.

A coffee room, opened in April 1887, was later augmented with a small restaurant, the first in a Canadian store. Shoppers could conveniently refresh themselves with a cup of coffee or tea and a bite to eat without having to leave the store. This copied similar facilities in large American department stores, and was a genteel way to encourage customers to remain on the premises. In a radical step taken to further entice women shoppers, Timothy Eaton started the practice of hiring female buyers. The women were dispatched to Eaton's European buying offices in London, Paris and Vienna to scout the latest fashions. In the early 1900s, women buyers were virtually unheard of, but the venture proved very successful. Women knew what women wanted.

The store boasted many firsts. Eaton's was the first Canadian store to feature electric lights. The first telephone system was installed in the store in 1884, and became for a brief time the largest retail telephone system in the world, handling up to 100,000 calls a day in Toronto alone. Elevators in the Queen Street store were met with some mistrust when they were first installed despite the fact that store management placed wax dummies in the elevators to demonstrate their safety; it was a week before customers decided it might be safe to rise 65 feet above ground level in a moving metal box. Later, Eaton's installed the first escalator.

Eaton's opened a 16-foot counter in the Queen Street store's drug department, where three attendants dispensed cold sodas and ice cream to wilting customers during the summer months. Dairy cattle, raised on the family's beautiful farms in Georgetown and Islington, provided the milk. The Islington farm was situated on 400 acres near what is now the busy junction of Highways 5 and 27. This area is still known as Eatonville, and a local public library bears this name.

This arrangement was the genesis of a close association between Eaton's restaurants and food services and the Eaton farms.

THE T. EATON Co. LIMITED

190 Yonge St. Canada's Greatest Store. Toronto.

DAIRY LUNCH ROOM.

BILL OF FARE.

Plate of Chicken or Duck.... .... 10 Cts.
Plate of Meat, Ham, Tongue or Beef 5 "
Hot Meat Pies (Harry Webb's)..... 5 "
Bread " " ..... 2 "
Butter (Eaton's Dairy).... .... 2 "
Bath Bun and Butter (Eaton's Dairy) 3 "
Tea Biscuits " .... 3 for 5 "

10C. LUNCH
Bath Bun and Butter, Glass of Milk and Ice Cream.

15C. LUNCH
Plate of Meat (or Meat Pie) with Bread and Butter, Glass of Milk and Ice Cream.

20C. LUNCH
Plate of Meat (or Meat Pie) with Bread and Butter, Pie or Cake, Glass of Milk and Ice Cream.

Cocoa per cup .... 5 Cts.
Tea or Coffee per cup, with Cream . 5 "
(State when Cream is not required.)
Milk per glass (Eaton's Dairy)...... 2 Cts.
Buttermilk " " ...... 2 "

ICE CREAM AND CAKE, 8 CTS. **ICE CREAM (EATON'S DAIRY), 5C.**

PASTRY.

Lemon or Fruit Pie (Harry Webb's).. 5 Cts.
Cream Puffs " .. 5 "
Jam Turnovers " .. 5 "
Small Tarts (Harry Webb's) 2 for 5 Cts.
Plate of Cake " .. 5 "
Walnut Tartlets " 2 for 5 "

ICE CREAM SODA, any of the following Flavors, **5 CTS.**

Strawberry, Raspberry, Coffee, Orange Phosphate, Peach, Vanilla, Chocolate, Nectar, Pine Apple, Cherry, Ginger, Lemon Phosphate.

Plain Soda, any above flavors, ... 3 Cts. Glass.

FRUITS IN SEASON.

Peaches and Cream.............. 7 Cts. | Sliced Oranges.................. 5 Cts.

SUNDRIES.

PANCAKES AND SYRUP, 5 CTS. | Jersey Butter (from our own Creamery), 25c. lb.

DAIRY FARMS AT ISLINGTON AND GEORGETOWN. (Over).

Menu, 1903

Mr. Eaton's imagination leaped to the pleasant prospect of an Eaton Farm. With little ado, he set out with the manager of the drug department . . . and after inspecting various properties, purchased at Islington a farm stocked with twenty cows. Henceforth, the ice cream and ice cream sodas were made from the cream produced under the Store's own auspices. At the end of the season, however, the farm produced also a problem: what to do with the cream in cold weather? The aforesaid manager suggested oyster stew. It was decided to try it. An unused portion of the basement was whitewashed, mirrors hung on the walls, and tables, chairs and cooking apparatus installed. The public evinced their appreciation of the idea by consuming about 500 bowls of stew a day — 10¢ a bowl with a few biscuits. Shortly afterwards, a slice of pie was put on the menu — 5¢ extra. Finally the cups of tea which were then being served upstairs at one side of the light well were brought down to bear company to the soup and pie, this leading gradually to the institution of a 25¢ dinner. (Golden Jubilee, pages 57-58*)*

Grill Room waiting area, May 24, 1911

By 1899, there was a lunchroom on the fifth floor of Toronto's flagship Queen Street store, offering shoppers a 20¢ lunch. By 1901, this location had expanded to occupy 22 acres of prime land in the Yonge and Queen area. As part of the store's overall expansion, the restaurant, which had been in the basement, was moved up to the fourth floor and improvements were made. A booklet entitled *The Home Comers*, published by Eaton's in 1903, informed shoppers that the fifth floor lunchroom served full-course breakfasts from 8 to 11:30 a.m., dinner from 11:30 a.m. to 2 p.m., and "hot and cold lunches all

The Grill Room, Queen Street store, 1910

day." The lunchroom served more than 5,000 customers daily. A menu dated October 24, 1904, advertised a 25¢ dinner. For an extra 5¢, a diner could order a baked apple with cream. From 3 to 5 p.m. a "dainty lunch" was available for 13¢; dainty lunch for two could be ordered for 25¢. This menu offered chicken salad with mayonnaise dressing, bread and butter, cake and ice cream, and tea or coffee. Cake counters and a soda fountain were located both on the main floor and in the basement of the Queen Street store. A splendid new marble-topped soda fountain was built on the store's main floor in 1904, and a tea room was added on the second floor.

Cafeteria, fifth floor, Queen Street store, c. 1910

In 1907, the fifth floor Grill Room was opened with semi-private dining rooms attached to the main room. The Grill Room entertained patrons with an orchestra and seated 450 people within its 25,000 square feet. This, and the managers' lunchrooms, often served 5,500 patrons a day. The cafeteria and a "quick lunchroom" occupied the basement. That year, the store also expanded to include employee cafeterias in the Eaton's Annex and other Eaton's buildings close to the flagship store. The utilitarian cafeteria, with 500 seats and very affordable fare, often served 5,000 people per day.

Queen Street store kitchen, 1904

Grill Room diners consumed up to 2,500 pounds of beef per week. The store's soda fountain and the basement lunchroom, which could accommodate 200 diners, used 1,200 gallons of ice cream each week, as well as 540 gallons of milk. To prepare and serve these staggering amounts of food to hungry patrons, there were 260 restaurant staff in the Queen Street store, including chefs, bakers and waitresses.

Queen Street store
fifth floor bakery, 1904

A visiting journalist, "H.S.H," described a visit to Eaton's Queen Street store for his British readers:

The Grill Room astonished me. One might be in some old hotel in England. Surrounded by oak walls and shelves, with artistic blue china vases on them, the tables are perfectly laid, and a waiter will bring you a fricassee, new potatoes, new corn on the cob with butter, deep Lawton berry pie, whipped

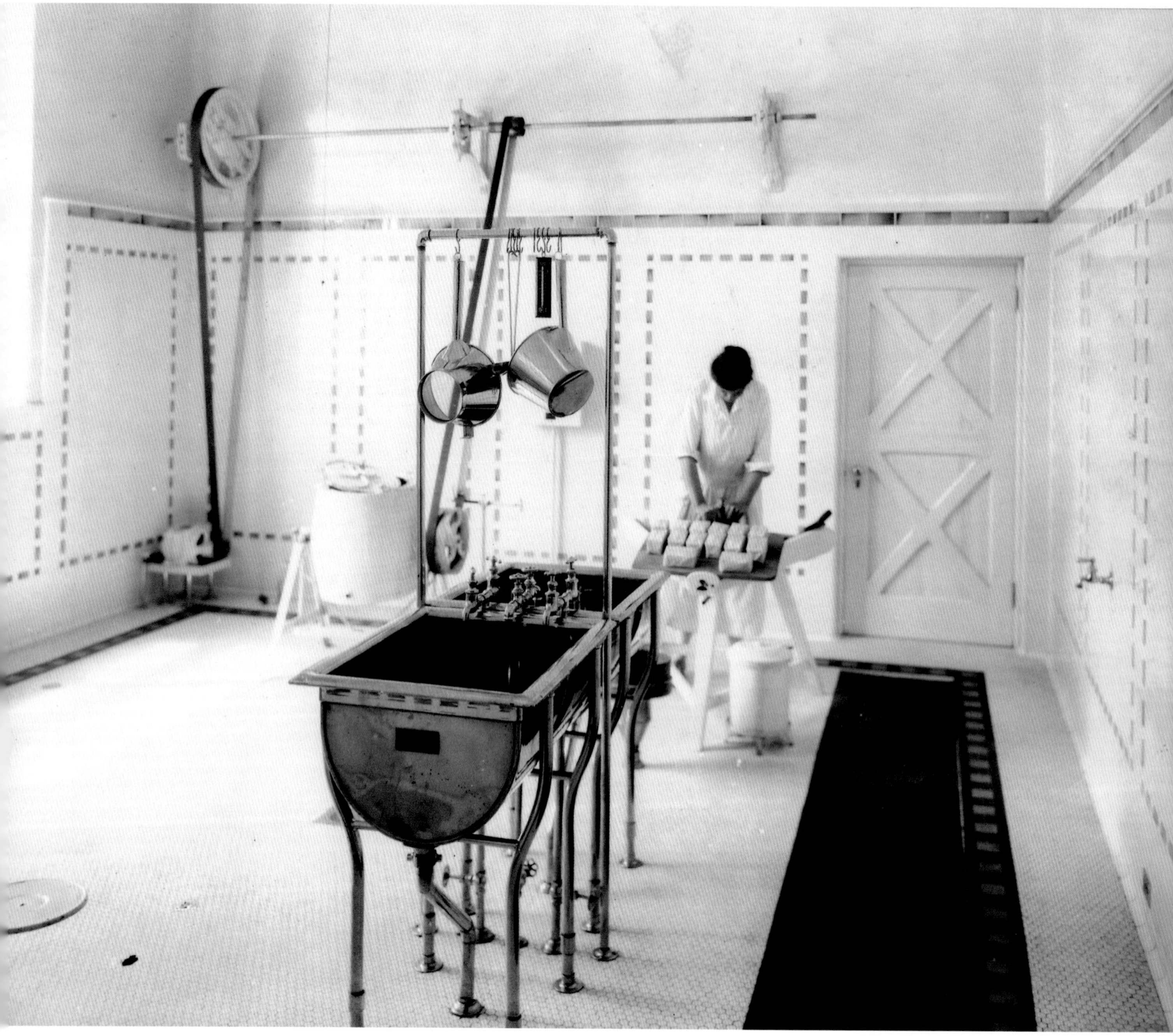

Woman in the dairy cutting butter, July 1923

cream and coffee, and, in the season, peaches, watermelon or ice cream for another 10¢, while an orchestra enables you to talk to your friends without being heard by others. (The Sunday World, September 10, 1907*)*

In the kitchen, which the journalist found "delightfully clean," he observed the chefs preparing cakes and pancakes to be eaten with maple syrup. He also discovered that each of the 170 2½-pound loaves of bread produced every day in the bakery were consumed on the premises. He went on to describe the scene in the dairy, where every day by 10 a.m. 600 to 650 pounds of fresh butter were churned and ready for sale. They were all sold by noon.

GREEN SEAL

A Hole in the Ground So Big . . .

Eaton's Winnipeg store opened on July 15, 1905. The occasion was a major civic event, presided over by Timothy and Margaret Eaton; Flora McCrea Eaton; her husband, John Craig; and their two-year-old son Timothy, who sat on his grandfather's knee while the three generations of Eatons rang the bell to open the store for a preview. Thousands of curious Winnipeggers rushed in for an hour-long inspection of the new premises.

At 1 p.m. on opening day, the Eatons hosted a celebratory luncheon, attended by representatives of Winnipeg business, the railway and the church. The Mayor of Winnipeg gave a congratulatory speech and the atmosphere was jubilant. John Craig Eaton was especially exultant, for overseeing this new venture in Winnipeg was his first

Cooking school in connection with Winnipeg grocery (in the dining room), c. 1905

major business responsibility. He had spent the previous two years consumed with its construction and set-up. The afternoon bell rang at 2:30 p.m., signalling the Eaton ladies to their posts: Mrs. Margaret Eaton as a floor-walking supervisor, Florrie McCrea in the Ribbon Circle as a salesgirl. The Eaton men grumbled that they were denied a similar opportunity to earn wages. The women were each paid 50¢, the going hourly rate. Lady Eaton kept her paycheque from this occasion as a souvenir.

Timothy Eaton worried that his son's enthusiastic projections for the Winnipeg store, which covered an entire city block (266 by 590 feet), had overestimated the market's need. The location of the site itself was worrisome as well, for although John Craig felt it had unlimited promise, it was half a mile west of the downtown core, and, in the early 1900s, nothing but a sports field lay beyond it. In the first stages of construction, Timothy Eaton was advised, not very reassuringly, by a business associate and friend that the excavation for the building was "a hole in the ground so big that it will never be needed in my lifetime or yours."

Despite initial anxiety about building it on the Portage Street site, at a cost of $350,000, the Winnipeg store was an instant success. In the space of a few months the staff doubled, growing from 700 to 1,300 to deal with the brisk trade. Within two years, the originally projected sixth storey was added to the store. By 1906, there were

plans to extend the store along Donald Street, adding a new entrance, a broad interior staircase, four new elevators and a marble soda fountain. The store also included a churning department where shoppers could obtain free samples of butter. Of the 250 trained Eaton's staff who had been sent out from Toronto to open and guide the new store, the majority remained in Winnipeg, entranced by the city's open, friendly spirit.

Employees' picnic at Elm Park, June 12, 1906: "Believed to be [the] first affair for Winnipeg managers."

To celebrate the Winnipeg store's success, a picnic was held on the first anniversary of the opening. This happy tradition continued into the 1920s.

On the first of July, a year after the Winnipeg opening (1905) a picnic was held at Portage la Prairie for the employees and their families. It was great fun, and Jack and I were glad we had made a special point of attending. On the 6th was the big anniversary celebration when the chief feature in the store was a huge cake adorned with the two dates in icing and one giant candle. Every customer that day was given a box of cake — and so successful was this birthday celebration that the same pattern has been followed on each anniversary since. (Memory's Wall, page 71*)*

The Winnipeg store's fifth floor lunchroom also opened in 1905, along with a main floor soda fountain. The cafeteria was enlarged within a month of the store's opening. The main restaurant, the Grill Room, the city's largest dining room, was often filled to capacity. Diners were drawn by its reasonable prices and excellent food and service. A stereoscopic photograph of the Winnipeg restaurant, one of a series produced by Eaton's in the early 1900s to advertise the store's many departments and features, bears this information:

Our lunch and grill rooms are on the fifth floor where you can obtain anything from light refreshment to a full-course dinner. These rooms have a combined seating capacity of a thousand, and an average daily patronage of from three to five thousand. The Grill Room is luxuriously furnished with Mission tables and chairs, tapestried walls and rugs. Visitors can inspect the kitchens on application to the Superintendent's office at any time.

Winnipeg lunchroom, 1910. One of a set of images of the Winnipeg store (to be viewed by stereoscope).

The 1910 Winnipeg edition of *The Story of a Store*, a promotional booklet published by Eaton's, advertised the attractions of the lunchroom: "Our lunchroom is for the convenience of customers. In it, at moderate cost, dainty luncheon and substantial meals. Our afternoon shoppers' lunch has become immensely popular. The kitchens connected with our grill and lunch rooms are splendidly equipped."

The restaurants were especially popular during the city's annual exhibition held in July. Winnipeggers and visitors to the city flocked to the Grill Room, with its oak panelling, beamed ceilings and iron chandeliers. English Minton china graced the tables and, in keeping with the genteel standards of the day, a string quartet entertained lunchtime diners. "To speak at any length of the Winnipeg Store is certain to evoke some mention of its Grill Room. It is a popular rendezvous for tourist and citizen alike. 'Let's go and have a piece of Mrs. Eaton's lemon pie' may be classed among the local bye-words" (*Golden Jubilee*, page 180).

The Winnipeg store very quickly became a main source of goods and services for Western shoppers. Much of the population of Canada west of Winnipeg lived on farms and in small communities, making

The Family Grocery Assortment

3	cans plums
3	cans peas
2	oz. nutmeg
2	oz. essence of lemon
4	oz. vanilla
7	lbs. marmalade
3	lbs. cornstarch
6	cans corn
1	lb. baking powder
3	cans catsup
3	cans raspberries
1	lb. pepper
3½	lbs. starch
7	lbs. rice
6	lbs. figs
5	lbs. raisins
7	lbs. dried peaches
6	lbs. currants
2	lbs. fruit peel
3	lbs. baking soda
½	lb. pastry spice
5	lbs. tea or coffee

the Winnipeg branch of Eaton's a major mail-order distribution centre for Western Canadian catalogue sales. The large and constant volume of mail-order business in the West buoyed Eaton's viability as a national commercial dynasty. The catalogue offered an extensive and fascinating variety of goods large and small for farm and domestic use. One story tells of a young farm wife who harnessed her team of horses by comparing it with the catalogue advertisement photo of the same when she had to rush her injured husband to the doctor. Some of Eaton's mail-order trade was in food. In 1910, for instance, the Family Grocery Assortment was available for $10. The list suggests how housewives of the day might have augmented locally available products with baking materials, dried and canned goods, and condiments ordered from Eaton's catalogue.

Residents of small towns in Manitoba, northwestern Ontario, the Northwest Territories and Saskatchewan thought of

Winnipeg store postcard c. 1930: "The largest retail organization in the British Empire."

Winnipeg as "the big city." Eaton's was *the* major shopping emporium north of the United States-Canada border. The store also served an important, if secondary, function as a centre of education, offering eager customers detailed instruction about how to use new products. Through promotions and demonstrations, patrons learned how to use everything from electric cookers and sewing machines to powdered foods and canned goods, how to preserve fruits and vegetables, and how to correctly set a table. Eaton's Winnipeg cookery schools, while primarily intended to promote new products, provided an important source of information to housewives about new foods and cooking methods.

S.FOSTER LTD

Licence Plate Number One

Flora McCrea had grown up in the town of Omemee, near Peterborough, Ontario, and had been the youngest of eight children. Her father, John McCrea, was a skilled woodworker and her mother, Jane, had a sweet soprano voice, a gift that Flora inherited. As a young woman, Flora McCrea had moved to Toronto to train as a nurse at Toronto General Hospital, where she was quickly asked to leave the profession. Undaunted, and determined to pursue her goal, she took a training position at Rotherham House, a private Toronto hospital where John Craig Eaton, fondly known by family and friends as "Jack," had been a patient. He was instantly captivated by Flora's kindness and forthright beauty. Though only 20 when they met, and despite her youth and inexperience, Flora gave no indication she was

Lady Eaton climbing into the new "Bluebird" Rolls Royce.
"Deacon at the wheel, gentle holding the door."

awed by the attentions of a handsome son of a well-to-do family. Both the McCreas and the Eatons had emigrated from Ireland, and the families had similar histories.

After a breathless courtship, Jack asked a reluctant John McCrea (he worried that a life of luxury would not be good for his daughter) for his consent to marry Flora. The McCreas announced their daughter's engagement on March 23, 1901. Though he came from a prominent family, Jack felt at ease with the informal Omemee way of life, and so the couple married at noon on May 8, 1901, in a simple ceremony at Omemee's Wesleyan Methodist Church. The Eaton family travelled to Omemee for the occasion by special train.

Flora McCrea's wedding gown was a high-necked, drop-shouldered, shirred and flounced creation of white chiffon over white taffeta. She carried a bouquet of her favourite blooms — white roses, lily of the valley and white heather. The plain church building was decorated for the occasion with stands of American Beauty roses and massed calla lilies. The wedding reception was held in the McCrea home and catered by the Toronto firm of Webb's, though the couple's wedding cake was made locally by McPherson's Bakery. As was customary at the time, small boxes of cake, accompanied with cards announcing the couple's names and the date of their marriage, were delivered to friends who had been unable to attend.

Lady Eaton had adjusted to her new role as wife, saying, "For the first time I was complete mistress of a household, planner of menus and cook too. Within a few days I discovered what was to be a guiding rule for the rest of my home-making career — that my husband liked plain, substantial, well-cooked food, such things as chops and rice pudding, and was inclined to suspect any of my attempts at variation" (*Memory's Wall*, page 47).

Early in their marriage, Mrs. Timothy Eaton lent her son and daughter-in-law her Muskoka summer home, Ravenscrag, on Lake Rousseau. In 1906, Flora and John Craig bought a log cabin, naming it "Kawandag," an Ojibway word meaning "meeting place of the pines," for the white pines that surrounded it. Starting with four acres of land, they gradually acquired an expansive property with 3,500 feet of shoreline, and built a two-storey summer home. With its white pillars and portico, Kawandag became a landmark at the rocky north end of Lake Rousseau. Lady Eaton sustained her love of entertaining while there, and was in the habit of inviting the nearby villagers to cricket matches and weekly songfests, which she led. At times, she invited musicians from Toronto to join in the Kawandag musical soirées.

The Eaton family grew with the birth of Timothy Craig in 1903 and as the family and the business grew, so did the Eaton's need for a larger Toronto home. In 1908, they bought a house called Ravenswood near Casa Loma and Spadina House. On that property, John Craig built Ardwold, Irish Gaelic for "high green hill." He surprised Flora with the completed new family home on her return from an extended family trip to Europe. The splendid, Georgian-style mansion stood on a high prospect from which the Eaton family looked out over the fountain and formal gardens to the city below. The house had 50 rooms, 14 baths, a half-acre glassed-in area enclosing a conservatory and swimming pool, and included a hospital wing. Though Ardwold no longer stands, a vestige remains; Ardwold Gate, which winds along the top of the hill near Casa Loma, was the former driveway up to the house.

The gardens, boasting fine ferns, orchids, chrysanthemums and caladiums, regularly won awards. Ardwold's grounds were also the site of many large-scale events. A May Festival held there featured "woodland revels, historic episodes of spring from the time of Morris dancers, Druids, Robin Hood, the crowning of the May Queen, with an audience of a thousand people, songs, sword play, and dancing around the May Pole" (Eaton's Archives). Recalling a reception given by their neighbours, the Austins — namesakes of the present-day Austin Terrace — Lady Eaton describes the scene:

. . . all the ladies in long dresses of satin or broadcloth, set off with fur stoles and occasionally a muff; a uniformity of kid gloves and feather-trimmed hats. How one managed all this plus a cup of tea and other things, I can't quite remember, yet I know we all did — keeping our gloves on throughout. A fruit punch was often served, and sometimes it was flavoured with brandy, but liquor or cocktails were never offered to afternoon guests in Toronto homes at that time. The only exception was made during the Christmas season when trays of Madeira or sherry would be passed to accompany the traditional Christmas cake. Normally the emphasis would be on elaborate refreshments such as marzipan cakes shaped to resemble flowers, vegetables and fruits, and other richly decorated delicacies. (Those, of course, were the days before dieting was heard of or practiced.) Some hostesses preferred to be non-conformist — and I remember Mrs. Beatty of Queen's Park declare that, as only acquaintances *came to afternoon receptions, she served just simple sandwiches and cake, reserving her major culinary efforts for luncheons or dinners at which she entertained her friends. (Memory's Wall,* pages 107–108*)*

Events, however, were not always held at the family home. A photograph taken on February 16, 1910, captures an opulent banquet at Toronto's King Edward Hotel. The dinner was held during a visit

Banquet at the King Edward Hotel, February 16, 1910.
Flora McCrea, John Craig Eaton, Margaret Eaton centre foreground.

by "Uncle John," Margaret Eaton's brother, and was hosted by Eaton's store managers in honour of John Craig Eaton, Mr. John Beattie and A.A. Gilroy, manager of the Winnipeg store. An inscription on the photograph describes the occasion:

Covers were set for eighty-four, tables being arranged in the form of a large diamond to represent the firm's trademark. Within the enclosure a grotto covered with moss and flowers supported a crouching beaver. Electric lights on each side of the grotto picked out a giant letter "E." Gorgeous floral effects with orchids and lilies adorned the tables on which an excellent menu was served. An orchestra almost hidden by the floral décor rendered selections of music during the banquet after which a program of entertainment was provided, interspersed with short speeches . . . Mrs. Timothy and Mrs. John Craig Eaton received bouquets of American Beauty roses.

Lavish entertainments were often accompanied by lavish gifts. Sir John was known for his impulsive generosity and often offered unexpected gifts — a motorcar, a mink coat — to management staff and their wives. Jack Eaton was a high-spirited, energetic man with a love of speed and travel. He and Lady Eaton enjoyed many adventures together, and many "firsts." Sir John was the proud possessor of Canada's first motorcar licence plate Number One. He was often seen at the wheel of a car, and on one occasion drove the future King George VI on a tour of Toronto. They owned a number of Rolls

Eaton's candy factory workers, 1919: upper left, Miss McGowan; centre front, Miss Caulfield, the workroom supervisor

Royces, naming the first three of them Bluebird, Yellowbird and Ladybird. Lady Eaton managed a few automotive firsts of her own: "She insisted on driving her husband's Winton Phaeton, the first automobile owned in Canada, and became the first lady driver in an accident. She said later the tiller of the elegant runabout was sluggish when she bashed through the closed ornamental gate of Miss Veale's School for Young Ladies at Bloor Street and Bedford Road" (*Toronto Star*, July 10, 1970).

Photograph of Ardwold taken by family friend Billy Bishop and signed "with Xmas greetings 1919 W.A. Bishop and G. Barker"

But it was not just land vehicles that captivated the Eaton's sense of adventure and travel. While the Eaton's third son Edgar was still young, Sir John bought a mahogany runabout, the *Florence*. On the family's first trip to Quebec City in 1913, two-year-old Edgar became seriously ill and was briefly paralyzed, possibly from drinking contaminated milk. Lady Eaton disembarked the *Florence* on its return from Quebec and never again set foot on the boat. Though Edgar recovered, the consequences of his illness were lasting and he was a convalescent for many months.

Lady Eaton, however, continued to travel with "The Court," her entourage of children, governesses, maids and nurses. The Eatons toured in Europe for business — Eaton's operated buying offices in

Paris, Zurich, Belfast, London and other centres — and often for pleasure. They were passengers on the maiden voyage of the *Lusitania*, and were aboard the first passenger-service flight in Canada. As guests of their friends Colonel Billy Bishop and Colonel Barker, the Eatons took a round-trip flight on the *Bishop Barker Flying Boat* between the Royal Muskoka Hotel and Toronto. The journey took an hour and 50 minutes.

Lady Eaton was susceptible to stress and exhaustion as her family grew. Following her doctor's orders to rest, she undertook a fishing trip to New Brunswick in 1917. She was accompanied by Annie Pringle, a friend who was also a talented amateur photographer, two guides and a cook. The two women took a relaxed approach to their appearances during their holiday, and Lady Eaton recalled that when her husband came to visit her — also hoping to catch some salmon, "Jack hardly knew me, I was so hot and red, and greasy with fly dope" (*Memory's Wall*, page 125). Industrious even while officially resting, Lady Eaton kept a journal and wrote an account of this journey along the Miramichi Valley. She copyrighted the book as *Rippling Rivers: My Diary*. One of the 255 original copies of this bucolic memoir went to the British Museum.

Lady Eaton also sang (she had inherited the talent from her mother) at home, in school choirs, and at church. Lady Eaton studied voice when her family commitments allowed, and, in 1920, made her debut as a concert singer, sharing a program with the Metropolitan Opera tenor Edward Johnson, who later became governor of the Royal Conservatory of Music. Johnson was a close family friend and persuaded Lady Eaton to sing the benefit concert with him, though her daughter Florence Mary was only five months old at the time.

The musical evening took place at Massey Hall. Lady Eaton wore a dress of blue and silver brocade with a long train. For the occasion, her husband had given her a tiara adorned with maple leaves made of diamonds, which she chose not to wear, as it had not been fitted. Later she had the tiara's diamonds fashioned into a maple leaf brooch; it became one of her favourite pieces of jewellery. Sir John also gave his wife a good-luck bracelet with the first bar of her first song set in diamonds and black enamel.

Despite her worry, the concert was a success, raising $6,000 for the visually impaired. Concert reviews praised the simplicity and unaffectedness of the groups of English, Irish, Italian and German songs Lady Eaton had chosen and described her voice as a pure soprano of rare sweetness. She went on to sing benefit concerts in a number of Canadian cities. Lady Eaton continued to study singing in Canada and in Europe, though she later expressed regret that she had come to singing too late to truly excel.

These years were a period of seemingly boundless expansion, prosperity and domestic happiness for the Eaton family, who had witnessed the birth of their children Timothy Craig in 1903, John David in 1909, Edgar Allison in 1911, Gilbert McCrea in 1915, and Florence Mary in 1919. An adopted daughter, Evlyn Beatrice, later joined the family.

The couple provided not only for their own family but also for the young men and women in their employ. Lady Eaton took a close interest in the lives and careers of young women who worked for the store. A minimum wage of $6 per week had been established for first-class sales women. Once they turned 18, many young women came from small towns to the city to take up clerking positions. For most, this was their first job and first time away from home and family; many were vulnerable to exploitation. Eaton's was a relatively benevolent employer and gradually cut back work hours to an average of 43 to 48 hours per week. Lady Eaton also established a mentoring network for young women, the Eaton's Women's Society, which reached out to some 18,000 girls and women. Lady Eaton wanted every young woman who came to work for the store to have someone to whom she could readily turn for advice or assistance.

Named for Timothy Eaton's wife, Toronto's Margaret Eaton School of Literature and Expression kept the livelihoods of women in mind as one of the first places where women could work toward careers other than secretarial or in retail. Young women studied elocution, movement and drama while at the school. Dora Mavor Moore, after whom the prestigious Dora awards for outstanding achievement in the performing arts in Toronto are named, was an early graduate. After the school amalgamated with the women's faculty of physical education at the University of Toronto, Eaton's Girls' Club members continued to use the swimming pool and other facilities at the McGill Street school, and female employees often had meals in the upstairs dining room.

Eaton's also established camps where young men and women could find recreation during the summer. Shadow Lake, a 200-acre property near Stouffville, northeast of Toronto, allowed employees to spend a week of summer holidays there for $5. The camp was on a farm, and the food was fresh and plentiful, supplied by the farm's dairy herd, chickens and a large market garden. For recreation, there was swimming, diving, riding and sailing. Eaton's also started boys' and girls' clubs, where young employees could study all manner of subjects, from cooking to folk dancing.

During World War I, John Craig enforced a policy of continuing Eaton's salaries to active service men and women, and held jobs open for their return. Some 3,327 men from Eaton's Toronto and Winnipeg stores and foreign buying offices enlisted for service; their wartime salaries were in the order of $2 million. Eaton supported the country's war effort in other ways as well — one of these was his $100,000 endowment of the Eaton Machine Gun Battery. In a further act of civic generosity, he arranged prompt and massive aid following the devastating Halifax harbour explosion in 1917, and travelled to the city to take part in the relief effort himself.

John Craig was knighted in the autumn of 1919 for his outstanding contributions to Canada's cause during World War I. The Duke of Connaught, who was then Governor General of Canada, performed the ritual of investiture. His wife, Princess Alice, became a lifelong friend of Lady Eaton's. On this momentous occasion, Lady Eaton was in a "state of exalted flutter" and heard the Duke's ceremonial command to her husband — "Arise, Sir Knight" — with tears of pride in her eyes.

Luncheon was served following the ceremony. Guests were seated at three large round tables in the dining room, each presided over by one of the Connaughts. Lady Eaton joined the Duchess' table, while

Sir John sat beside the Connaughts' daughter, Princess Patricia. The group stood for a military grace. Royal meals were not permitted to be longer than an hour; if the party paused to put their forks down, hapless diners had their unfinished courses whisked away.

In the winter of 1922, at the age of 46, and after two decades of service to the Eaton family and store, Sir John died suddenly of pneumonia, following a bout of the flu.

I Began to Dream of Something Better

Following both her husband's and her father-in-law's death, Lady Eaton stepped forward to take the reins of the company, continuing the efforts begun by Sir John to entice the "carriage trade" with fine goods and services. Along with this refocusing on higher-end clientele, she reconsidered the profile of the store's restaurants.

Timothy Eaton had taken Flora McCrea on his daily rounds of the Toronto store, and had solicited her thoughts about business matters. Lady Eaton attributed her knowledge of the business to observations made during this time. It had been customary in the early 1900s for businessmen to return home for lunch, but when Timothy Eaton found that he needed to remain in the store to work, the idea of the "businessman's lunch" was born. In a handwritten speech among her

Georgian Room with organ, 1924

Portrait of Lady Eaton, August 1928, taken for Who's Who

effects at Eaton Hall, Lady Eaton cited this shift as the genesis of Eaton's restaurants:

Sometimes he [Timothy Eaton] felt pressed for time and would want to remain down at the store for lunch rather than drive home and back again. In the grocery department, tea, bread, butter, milk, eggs, cold meats and cheese were sold. At first he would have a sandwich and a cup of tea in his office. Finally, an electric broiler came out. Someone showed it to him. He thought it an excellent idea. He had three tables put in a corner of the grocery department and then he had a broiled steak or a chop and fried potatoes for his lunch. Soon a table was set up where the customer could get sandwiches, tea, coffee and milk, cake and pies. From that necessity of his was born, in a simple way, the forerunner of the Snack Bar of today, and the fine restaurants which we have from coast to coast. (Lady Eaton, speech to Bolton Rotary Club, 1952)

In addition, Lady Eaton's love of travel had allowed her to observe first-hand the appeal of stores and dining rooms in New York City as well as in England. London's Debenham's, Selfridges and Harrod's, and in New York City, the B. Altman Company and Lord & Taylor were her natural terrain. Eaton's kept track of merchandising trends,

Butter, eggs and cheese counter, August 1908, Queen Street store

product availability and design, as evidenced by the Eaton's business records, which include many photographs of sumptuous displays of goods offered in the great department stores of the era. Harrod's exquisite Georgian Restaurant may have served as the inspiration for that in Eaton's flagship Toronto store.

It is no wonder, then, that Lady Eaton began to entertain the idea of a modern restaurant, equipped with first-class equipment and food. When she became a member of Eaton's Board of Directors in 1921, one of Lady Eaton's particular responsibilities was the reorganization of the store's restaurants.

Butter-making, Toronto, July 19, 1919

I began to dream of something better. Toronto badly needed a new, good restaurant, and I was groping toward the kind that would attract women as well as businessmen. Other parts of the store were constantly being modernized, carefully equipped and stocked; lovely things from the world around came to our various departments; we had fashions from the best designers in Paris — but we still had a commonplace restaurant. On trips to New York and abroad I did some serious scouting. In London I was invited to have luncheon in the Directors' dining room of one of the big department stores. It was a beautiful room in the classic style: Chippendale furniture, fine Oriental rugs and brocade curtains. The table appointments were of the best; in fact, here was a dining room worthy of a fine home. With a shock I realized I could never ask this group of men to have lunch in our restaurant in Toronto! (Memory's Wall, page 145*)*

Lady Eaton brought forward the idea of a select restaurant to Eaton's Board of Directors at a meeting in 1922:

I presented my case to the Eaton Directors. I knew that what I wanted wouldn't be a cheap venture, but I felt strongly that it would be a profitable investment in the end. Alas, my suggestion was turned down; the plan was too costly, I was told, and actually wasn't "a business proposition." I said I was willing to accept the decision, but then added, 'Now I would like to ask a favour. I want you to close down the restaurant we have, for I am ashamed of it' . . . That afternoon the President, Mr. R.Y. Eaton, came to Ardwold to reopen the subject, on the advice of the other Directors who had continued to discuss the matter after the morning's meeting. I was reluctant to go along with this rather sudden change of thinking — it could happen that my dream would turn into a white elephant — but after two hours' intensive discussion I agreed to move ahead on the plan of designing a new restaurant service for the Toronto store. (Memory's Wall, pages 145–146*)*

Lady Eaton and Mr. Charles Boothe, an Eaton's manager, became the steering committee for the new restaurant. In a speech which Lady Eaton gave many years later, she recalled her insistence that they "must not even begin a plan without a competent head to take over the order, but more importantly still, to advise us as to how the machinery for perfect service should be installed" (Lady Eaton,

Georgian Room menu cover, 1930

speech to Bolton Rotary Club, 1952). She stressed that the restaurant must be unlike anything Eaton's had previously offered. When Mr. Boothe asked her how she proposed to accomplish this feat, Lady Eaton declared, "I'm going to try to get Violet Ryley" (*Memory's Wall*, page 146).

Violet Ryley was a dietitian, a new breed of scientist. Domestic science was an emerging field in Canada, pioneered by Mrs. Lillian Massey Treble, who had started teaching scientific housecraft in a Toronto King Street basement in 1896, and later founded the Faculty for Household Science at the University of Toronto. Violet Ryley, an ardent and talented young proponent of this new field, studied at the Lillian Massey School of Household Science. While Ryley was still a student, Lady Eaton had hired her to train domestic staff in food preparation and service. A woman of exceptional organizational ability and good taste, Miss Ryley quickly amassed an impressive breadth of experience. She inaugurated the food services at the University of Toronto's Hart House, and also worked at the Bigwin Inn on Lake

Muskoka, making it the first hotel food service in North America to be managed by a dietitian. Following World War I, Ryley served as chief dietitian for Canada's military hospitals. When approached by Mr. Boothe and Lady Eaton about the prospects of a new dining service for Eaton's, Miss Ryley had just retired from her work with the military.

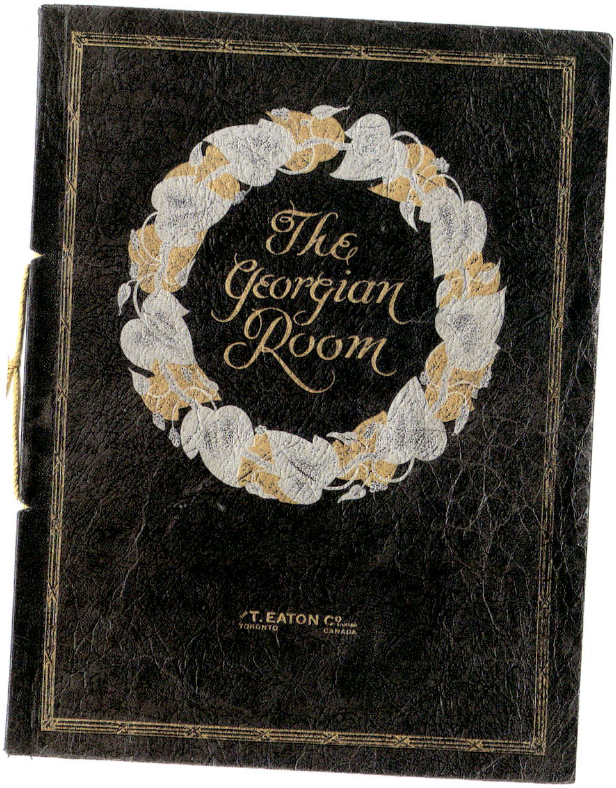

Georgian Room menu cover, 1940s

Mr. Boothe and I met Miss Ryley and won her immediate interest. We hastened to the next Board meeting with our report, and it was unanimously agreed that we could engage Miss Ryley. From that time forward she worked with us, preparing lists of requirements for kitchens and restaurant, consulting with René Cera, the Paris-trained architect who had joined the Eaton organization some time before. He drew the plans for this huge new restaurant floor remodelled at the top of the main store. For long hours together, Miss Ryley and I were immersed in the selection of linen, china, silver, waitresses' uniforms; we had frequent meetings with Mr. Boothe and the architect, and never was I associated with a more enterprising, or stimulating, or harmonious group of people. (Memory's Wall, page 146*)*

Georgian Room china mark: Minton china, made in England

Designer René Cera had joined Eaton's staff in the early 1920s. His ongoing influence as a member of Eaton's design and engineering department contributed to the overall transformation of the store meant to attract the carriage trade. Lady Eaton became an Eaton's vice-president in 1923. She insisted on the best of everything for the Georgian Room, as the original cost account for supplying china, service ware, linens and glassware attests:

Theodore Haviland china	*$ 9,868.95*
Linen	*$ 5,635.48*
Glassware	*$ 1,254.29*
Cutlery	*$ 4,734.21*
Hollowware (teapots, bowls, etc)	*$29,375.40*
Total	*$50,868.33*

Georgian Room china mark: Theodore Haviland, Limoges, France, used in Toronto and Winnipeg

The original tableware for the Georgian Room was Limoges china of a design specially created for the restaurant by

Theodore Haviland. Later, the English company Minton reproduced the design. Minton china in the Georgian Room pattern was used for the entire life of the restaurant. The pattern was described as a "mythical bird, blue body, beige plumage, sitting on mauve branches, green leaves, orange flowers border design, shades of beige and yellow all on white" (City of Toronto Archives).

"The Georgian Room, the name we had chosen because it so well suited the dignity of the first decorative scheme, opened in 1924. People close to the food industry in Canada have often stated that it revolutionized restaurant menus and service everywhere. Certainly it set a new, a quite different standard, and my cherished dreams were realized" (*Memory's Wall*, page 147). The Georgian Room opened on Monday, March 10, 1924. An Eaton's announcement of the opening reads:

Black demitasse, original Georgian Room ware

Round bread and butter plate and relish plates, original Georgian Room china

Georgian Room kitchen, May 3, 1924

You cannot fail to like the Georgian Room. Stepping from the elevators (the new group in the South Yonge St. section), you pass through a lobby into a vast room of beautiful proportions and architectural design. It is purely Georgian in design and decoration, with lofty twenty-four foot ceiling, high windows, and walnut panelling. At one end is a musician's gallery where an orchestra will play during lunch and afternoon tea. Blue and gold brocaded hangings, tall mirrors in the wall, cut crystal chandeliers and solid walnut chairs, upholstered in blue velvet, contribute beauty and dignity. The table appointments — fine Irish linen, Haviland china, and fine glass and silver — double the pleasure of lunching in these surroundings. But of even greater significance to guests will be the quality and excellence of the menu and the conditions in which the food is prepared. A glimpse 'behind the scenes' is enlightening. The new kitchen is unique. There is the uninterrupted height of two storeys. Thus it has excellent ventilation, and is flooded with light and sunshine. The equipment is the best and most complete that could be procured. The utmost importance is attached to the quality of the food. Only the best will be used, while the ingenuity of a chef with years of European and American experience, and the skill of expert dietitians, will combine in providing a menu attractive, well-balanced and perfectly presented.

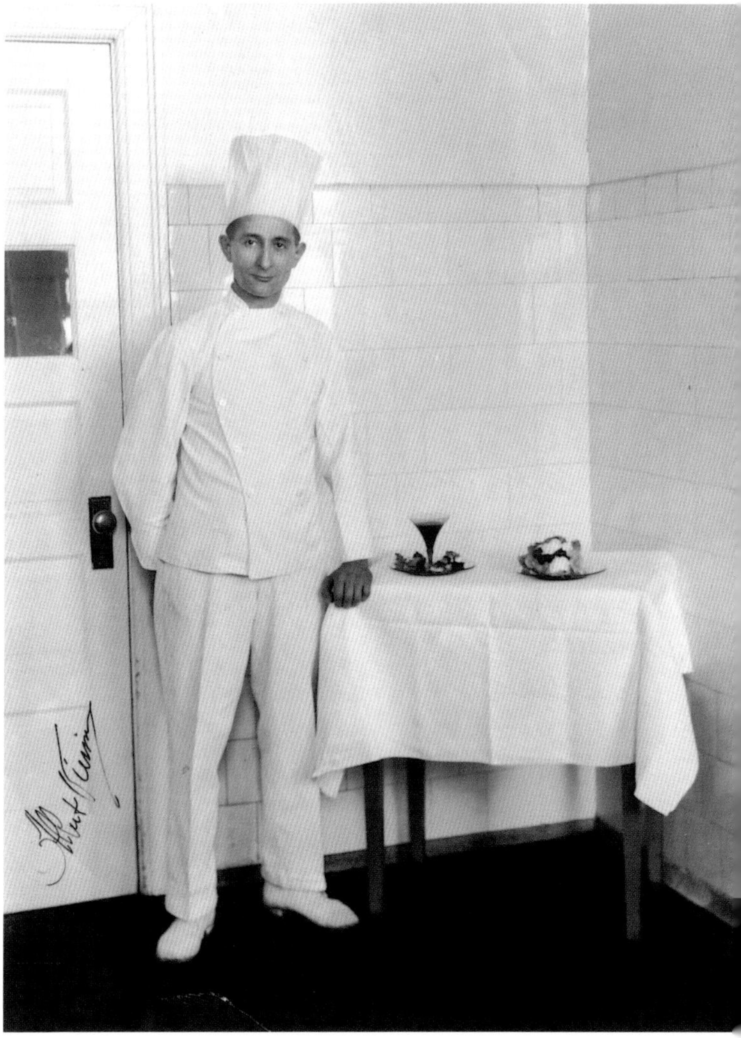

Albert Vierin, first Georgian Room chef, c. 1924

Miss Edith Macdonald, "the Scribe," who created publicity materials for the store at that time, wrote advertising materials for the

Georgian Room, full view, 1924

Watercolour of Chinese panel. It was one of a set of four bought by Lady Eaton and hung in both the Georgian Room and the Round Room.

Georgian Room, and described Lady Eaton's role as superintendent of the new dining room. Her influence regarding construction décor and the quality of all the room's fixtures was matched by the attention devoted to the preparation of attractive and perfectly balanced and presented meals. The Georgian Room, Miss Macdonald wrote, changed customers' habits. For the first time, it offered downtown shoppers an alternative to dining at the Royal York or King Edward Hotel, or in amateur tea rooms where meals consisted of unappetizing plates of meat and heaps of potatoes.

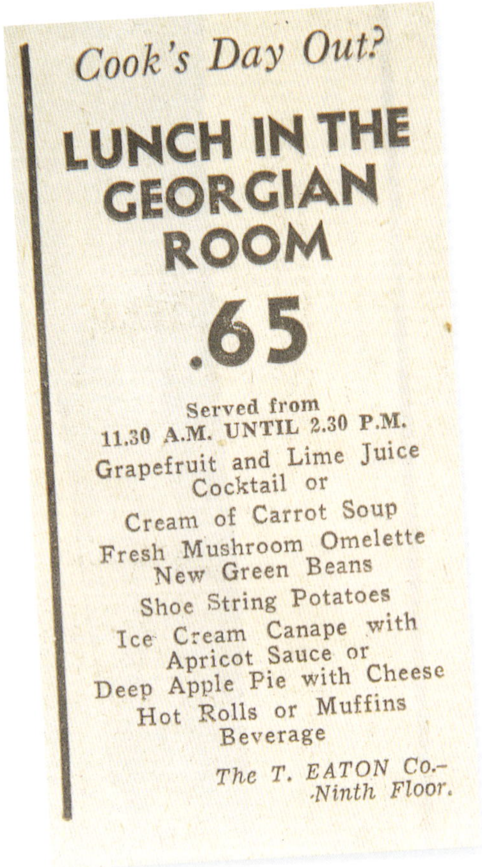

"Lunch in the Georgian Room" ad in The Evening Telegram, *Toronto, Tuesday, January 21, 1936*

Lady Eaton liked a personal touch, and to enhance the decoration of the Georgian Room she obtained four Chinese silk panels. Two large panels hung on each side of the passageway at the room's east end, leading to the kitchens. The Georgian Room created an aura of luxury and serenity. In its early days, an orchestra played at lunch and tea time, and there was a Hammond organ in the restaurant. At first the room's colour scheme consisted of off-white walls with mahogany trim. Miss Jean Hall, a dietitian in the Georgian Room's early days, remembered that later, the walls were painted pink, a decision that initially lost patrons. Later, the whole room was redone and the floor around the pillars raised, while the ceiling remained gold leaf. The waitresses' uniforms were always a significant part of the overall presentation of the restaurant. One new 1930s version of the Georgian Room waitresses' uniforms replicated those of waitresses at Lord & Taylor's upscale Manhattan dining room.

The Georgian Room proved a brilliant success for "fastidious lunching," the Scribe's ecstatic term for this new development in Canadian dining. The restaurant was popular both with ladies and with businessmen seeking a calm place to meet and socialize. By the end of the restaurant's first year, Eaton's directors sat at their own corner table each day at lunchtime, contentedly taking in the bobbing sea of women's hats, the lines of tables gleaming with pretty china, silver and glass — and the waitresses' trays in full bloom with Georgian Room creations called salad plates. "It was obvious that a dining service of this character would henceforth be an essential feature in all Eaton's big-city establishments" (*Shopkeepers to a Nation: The Eatons*, page 83).

The
Georgian Room
Hostess Shop

A Land of Plenty

Eaton's expansion continued throughout the 1920s. In Western Canada, Eaton's opened stores in Regina in 1926, in Saskatoon in 1928 and in Edmonton in 1929. The Calgary store, which opened in 1929, stood at 408 8th Avenue South West on the western edge of the city's downtown core. Construction took two years and cost $1 million. George Fordyce, a Calgary architect, was the local associate of Ross and Macdonald of Montreal, the architectural firm for the Montreal Eaton's.

Constructed of steel and reinforced concrete in Renaissance Revival style, the four-storey Calgary building featured a cladding of Tyndall limestone from the Eaton's Manitoba quarry, excellent for

Georgian Room Hostess Shop, c. 1926

carving the elaborate decorative detail that framed the display windows and cornices. Inside, the store was entirely finished in white plaster and marble, with tiled floors throughout. It featured five elevators as well as the city's first escalator, fitted with wooden treads, which carried passengers from the ground floor to the basement. In the basement, shoppers found the luncheonette, the cash-and-carry grocery department, and fresh meat and fruit. The Alhambra Tea Room, on the third floor, was a Moorish design, adding an exotic Spanish-Moroccan flavour.

The opening of a new Eaton's store was a noteworthy municipal event. Lady Eaton and her son Timothy opened the Calgary store on February 28, 1929, turning a special gold key in the lock to mark the occasion. The store had hired about 500 staff for the opening, while an estimated 5,000 shoppers flooded through the four main entrances in the first half hour.

In Winnipeg, a 1923 booklet titled *Facts About Eaton's* advertised:

The Grill Room — on the fifth floor — the ideal place for a quiet, well-served dinner, alone, with a friend or two, or an association banquet. Our Grill Room service is complete in everything that makes a good meal successful — food suited to your choice, cooked to your wishes, and served to your satisfaction in tastefully appointed surroundings. Arrangements can be made with the Grill Room office for special dinners. Seating capacity, 260 persons.

Winnipeg coffee bar, third floor, June 1938

A Grill Room orchestra played *"gay and sparkling music at lunch and tea hours"* while the adjoining cafeteria was *". . . a land of plenty for the one who wishes a downtown meal in quick time or a light breakfast or lunch. Hot and cold meats, vegetables, salad, and all kinds of confections are laid out attractively for the self-serve system. The seating capacity is 666."*

Facts About Eaton's extolled the low prices of the cafeteria and the attractions of the lunch counters and soda fountains on the main and third floors. Women shoppers were offered the use of a supervised children's playground on the rooftop of the store in summer, and an indoor playground in winter where families could leave baby carriages or

Window display, 1920s, advertising "Empire Shopping Week: Food Stuffs — products of a worldwide Empire"

sleighs while they did their shopping. In the baby shelter, as many as 130 infants were cared for on a busy shopping day, tended by a competent nurse.

Meanwhile, as well as feeding shoppers on the premises, the Winnipeg store did a huge trade in groceries in Eaton's extensive basement grocery department. As the city's profile changed with succeeding waves of immigration, the basement groceteria catered to many influences, Icelandic, French, Ukrainian and Kosher among them. With 50 kinds of local sausage on offer, the Winnipeg meat department counter was 200 feet long, the longest in North America, and at one time shipped steaks as far as Florida and Toronto. The

Eaton's Winnipeg pie studio, third floor, 1936, featuring "Malto, the Health Bread" and "Fresh Fruit Pies in Season: Plum, Green Apple, Peach"

butcher counter featured haggis year round. During the 1930s, the Winnipeg store boasted the largest area of refrigerated displays and food sales counters in Canada, if not on the entire continent. (The first supermarket opened in the United States in 1930. As supermarkets spread north they radically altered food-buying habits in Canada.)

The staff cafeteria was well laid-out and offered a variety of salads, soups and sandwiches, and the Winnipeg bakeries operated 22 hours a day, supplying the area within a 200-mile radius with 13 varieties of bread. The bakeries specialized in custom-decorated cakes for weddings and other special occasions. During the 1930s, Eaton's Winnipeg baker, Harry Anderson, was popular for his pies, potato cakes, English muffins and crumpets. Hundreds of fruit pies were produced in the bakery's modern electric oven.

Young winners of regional Boys' and Girls' Club competitions travelled to Winnipeg to witness the latest advancements in subjects, including bread-making, canning and preserving. By the 1930s, Eaton's Cooking School had earned a stellar reputation. The store's Hostess Shop also offered to cook gourmet meals for any number of guests, using a housewife's own kitchenware. This service included the recipes, in case guests complimented the hostess by asking for them. Such initiatives were considered part of the Winnipeg store's tradition, and were intended to draw customers and instruct the public in new developments, products and services.

Oriental coffee shop (located in the furniture annex) menu cover, 1928

In Ontario, the Hamilton Eaton's store opened in 1927. The restaurant, originally called the Pansy Room, was renamed the Green Room on May 20, 1933. The downtown store supported its restaurant service with a production kitchen and bakery, and later opened a Men's Grill. An Eaton's Men's Grill ad boasted that it was "mannish in every detail. The food is mannish too . . . tender, juicy steaks, savoury chops, country sausage, fish, chicken, salads . . . à la carte or featured on special luncheons at 50¢, 75¢ or $1.00." The Hamilton store also offered customers the Little Green Cake Counter, an ice-cream counter, and groceries, making Eaton's Hamilton store a preferred "one-stop-shopping" destination.

A branch of Eaton's was also opened in Huntsville, Ontario, in 1928, in part so that Eaton family members could shop while they were staying at the Muskoka cottage. Deliveries were made to summer homes by lake steamer as well as by ground transport, dropped off at cottage docks at no extra charge. Butter and other perishables were packed on ice to preserve them on the summer heat.

A CARD of "SPECIALS"
THAT YOU CAN ORDER CONVENIENTLY FROM
EATON'S FINE FOOD SERVICE
Phone ADelaide 5211
Dependable City and Suburban Delivery
Convenient and time saving—and above all satisfaction when ordering foods from EATON'S.—These specials will help you save on your week-end needs.
For Friday and Saturday Only March 8th and 9th
• Tender Fresh Garden Peas, canned for your convenience, Sieve No. 4.
Eatonia Choice Peas No. 2 Tin 2 Tins 21c
• Aylmer Brand—natural flavour condensed
Tomato or Vegetable Soup 3 Tins 20c
• Especially recommended for its strength of flavour,
EMPIRE COFFEE Ground Fresh Lb. Tin 37c
• Gold Buckle Brand fine flavoured Seedless
Large ORANGES Doz. 45c 2 Doz. 88c
• It's dated for freshness.—Breakfast style
Eatonia Rindless BACON Lb. 39c
• A natural unsweetened—refreshing drink,
Dole's Pineapple Juice 3 7-oz. Tins 25c
• Cut from the famous tender Diamond Baby Beef.
PRIME RIB ROAST English Style Lb. 23c
• Combination Special—1 bundle of
Celery Hearts Iceberg Head Lettuce Both for 28c
EATON'S Food Department, 5th Floor.
T. EATON C° LIMITED
TORONTO CANADA

A card of specials from Eaton's food services

A Halifax branch of Eaton's opened its doors in 1928. A large mail-order headquarters for the East Coast opened in Moncton soon after and remained a focal centre for the region for more than 40 years.

Crown Jewels

Lady Eaton continued her business commitments to Eaton's throughout the 1930s, dividing her time between Canada and extended sojourns abroad. Lady Eaton was especially fond of Italy, and she and her children took up residence in the Villa Natalia in Florence, a house originally built for Queen Elizabeth of Romania. She studied art and languages alongside her children. In an interview in 1929, Lady Eaton reflected that her family was her first priority: "My real business is to bring up a family. My music is a diversion. My position as head of the company is not my own choice, but has been thrust upon me, so to speak."

Influences from Lady Eaton's love of travel were seen in the Round Room, which opened in 1930. The Round Room was part of

Round Room flower show, 1939

Paris buying office picnic. Lady Eaton and Timothy Craig Eaton at right, May 31, 1923.

the grand design of Eaton's College Street store. The seventh floor restaurant, private dining rooms, lounges and the 1,500-seat Eaton Auditorium were all joined by the long foyer, which served as an occasional activity area. These rooms were designed to be reminiscent of the luxurious ocean liners of the day.

Eaton Auditorium, from the time it opened, was a Toronto cultural centre. Visiting musicians, actors, lecturers and singers performed there and contributed to the development of burgeoning local culture, as premiere performances like that of The National Ballet of Canada in 1951, attest.

The Round Room provided an elegant setting for fashion shows, flower shows, special presentations and promotions, debutante balls and cotillions. Men's coffee clubs were regulars in the restaurant. The Canadian Women's Club met at Eaton's College Street, and took tea at the Round Room after its meetings and lectures. Kiwanis music festivals regularly took place in the Eaton Auditorium, and children's choirs often breakfasted in the Round Room before their festival appearances.

Lady Eaton and John David Eaton opening the College Street store, October 1930

The College Street store was designed by the Montreal architectural firm of Ross and Macdonald, with associate architects Sproatt and Rolph. Jacques Carlu was charged with the interior design, taking responsibility for the suite of public rooms. Carlu, a French-born architect and designer who later designed the Rainbow Room for New York City's Rockefeller Center, was a professor of design at the Massachusetts Institute of Technology.

Customers heading for the Round Room took the green elevators from the east side of the ground floor up to the seventh floor, and entered the restaurant from the foyer through glass and Monel metal doors. The dining room, on the north side of the building, was a circle within a square, with recessed alcoves filling the corners.

Drawing of one of Denis Gelin's Round Room sculptures

Circular mouldings in the domed ceiling, and circles worked into the floor tiling, continued the round motif. "As in the Auditorium and Foyer, the colour scheme was silvered tones of beige and grey with black — but Carlu's restaurant interior is more refined and radiant, as if liberated by the shape of the room, with the curve of the ceiling ringed by a wide band of polished black glass and the 'dome' enamelled a sunny lemon yellow" (William Dendy, *Lost Toronto*, page 162).

Carlu's wife, Natacha, a visual artist, designed the murals integral to the restaurant's décor. They depicted life in the village, forest, fields, and by the sea. The paintings were installed on the four curved walls between the corner alcoves. Their idealization of country life, inspired by French design, was echoed in eight terracotta statuettes. Created by French sculptor Denis Gelin, these elongated peasant figures were white enamel and stood on either side of the alcoves in niches lined with polished black Carerra glass. Satin-finished metal was used for all the doors, trimming, ventilation grilles and lighting fixtures.

Round Room, full view, 1930s

[T}he focal point of the room was a circular fountain on a pedestal of circular black-and-frosted-glass plates, lit from below through the shimmering water. Placed around the fountain, like planets around the sun, were the tables, covered with white linen, and black sandalwood chairs with beige leatherette upholstery. Above the fountain, a chandelier of similar design hung from the dome of the ceiling; its lowest level was an enclosed radio speaker to provide music. These two elements — the lighted fountain and the chandelier with its radio — were symbols of a modernity that united grace and technology. Together, they epitomized the interior of the whole store, which combined forms borrowed from contemporary technology — like the exposed fluorescent lighting and the horizontal and vertical patterns of streamlining — with fine materials and craftsmanship, and transformed them into classic works of applied art. (William Dendy, *Lost Toronto,* page 162*)*

When it opened, the College Street store was acclaimed as the "crown jewel" of Eaton's empire. Although never completed because of the onset of the Depression, original plans for the new building included a 36-storey central tower that would have significantly altered the Toronto skyline.

A pamphlet published at the time of the opening proclaimed: "Beyond the grace of fine proportion which in every great architectural conception must have a universal appeal, there is the question of practical use. Here this majestic store is a veritable triumph. From the

Round Room table for two, 1930s

delivery of incoming merchandise to the designs and positions of the showcases; from the outside elevator service to the planning of the restaurant kitchens, the practical aspect has received as much consideration as the aesthetic" (*College Street — with our compliments,* 1930 promotional booklet).

Great pride was taken in the use of all-Canadian materials. Ivory Tyndall limestone from the Eaton's Manitoba quarry, black granite from Mount Johnson, Quebec, and polished brown granite from

> *Lady Eaton has required that coloured uniforms should be used in all departments as she is very much averse to black. The Round Room is one exception to this due to the moderne colour scheme. Professor Carlew [sic] required that a black one should be used to be in keeping with the room.*
>
> (Memo, September *17, 1934*, Miss Frieda Beithaupt, Round Room manager)

Gananoque were used in construction. Monel metal, a rustless alloy that required no polishing, was used throughout, and praised as an all-Canadian product which paid tribute to the beauty and practicality of modern invention.

Jacques Carlu was in control of all aspects of the Art Moderne design. All the furniture and decoration, including lighting fixtures, ventilation grilles, glassware, silverware and china were executed according to his sketches, or selected to promote overall harmony. At his request, the waitresses' uniforms were black, in keeping with the room.

The dishes for the Round Room were Royal Worcester china, white with four black rings around the edge. Original Round Room stemware was Fostoria glass. The goblets had a square black bottom, continuing the glass motif of the fountain.

The Round Room became a favourite with Lady Eaton. She often took tea there, preferring the relative privacy of the alcoves to the room's open central area. She favoured it for social occasions as well, and it became part of the public and private celebrations of the Eaton family. In her later years, Lady Eaton would often call the Round

Room to have lunch delivered to her while she was visiting the store's hairdressing salon.

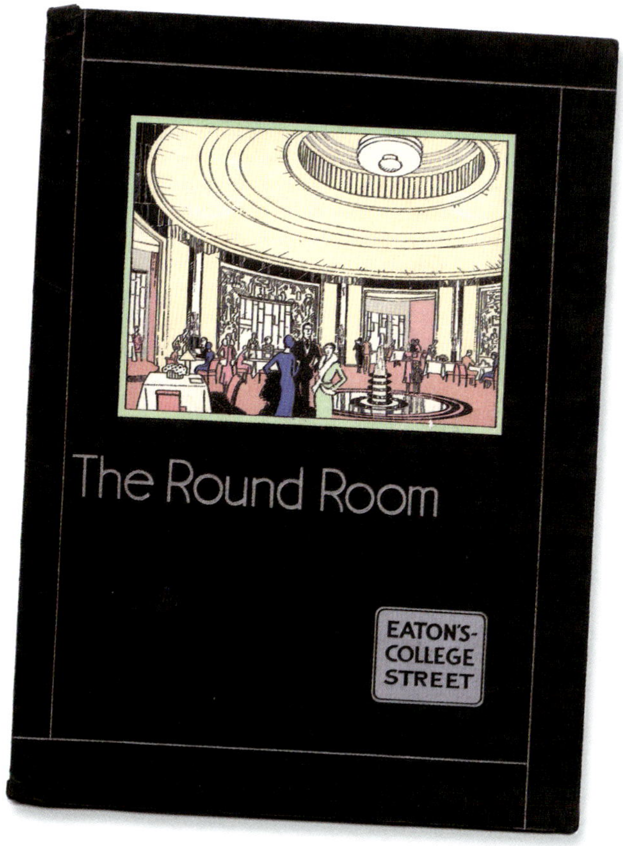

Round Room menu cover, 1930s

Eaton's bought a large property on Montreal's Ste. Catherine Street in 1925. Previously known as Goodwin's, the building was a handsome structure occupying an entire city block. While situated close to an invisible border between the French and English sections of the city, Eaton's was a destination for all, and the restaurant, known by locals simply as "The Ninth Floor," was a haven for women shoppers. Catherine Martin's charming film *The Ladies of the 9th Floor (Les dames du 9e),* made just before the Montreal dining room closed in 1998, reminds us of how few places there were in the 1930s to which respectable women could go alone.

The Montreal dining room was inspired by a transatlantic voyage Lady Eaton took on board the *Ile de France.* The ninth floor restaurant and foyer reflected the elongated formality of the ship's first-class dining room, designed by Carlu. The room was originally called François Premier, after a 15th-century French king, but the name did not catch on and the restaurant was simply known as Le 9e. It opened

Le 9e menu cover showing detail from Natacha Carlu's panels

on January 25, 1931. Jacques Carlu described his design for the ninth-floor Montreal room this way:

The central nave represents a clerestory ringed with horizontal windows admitting, through panels of opal glass, natural and artificial light well under control. The aisles are illuminated indirectly with light placed in inverted wells in the ceiling. The nave is surrounded with a range of columns of escalette brèche *marble in pink and soft grey, supporting the wall where*

Le 9e, close view, January 28, 1931

the clerestory windows are set. The lintels between the columns are decorated with bas-reliefs by Denis Gelin. At either end and along each side are two raised balconies with railings of Monel metal, reached by steps of black Belgian marble. The walls are covered with a horizontal striped French fabric, beige and pink. The floor is of Ruboleum tiles with an unusual pattern of colors. At both ends of the room are two huge vases of ceramics, resting on Belgian marble bases. These are illuminated from the inside. (The Architectural Record, Volume 69, #6, June 1931*)*

Le 9e menu cover, October 1934

The floor used seven shades of Scotch Ruboleum tiles, a material which, though the height of modernity in 1931, is no longer in use. *Escalette brèche*, a multicoloured marble quarried in the Pyrenees, was used as a complement to the room's black Belgian marble. Natacha Carlu's murals represented an "Amazonian Arcadia, one scene representing the Pleasures of the Chase, the other the Pleasures of Peace" (Eaton's publicity notes, 1939).

The restaurant, which initially seated 650, was appointed with fine, plain-bordered Irish linens, supplied by McCrum, Watson and Mercer of Belfast. English Royal Worcester china, glassware from Czechoslovakia and Germany, and Sheffield flatware completed the table settings. The staff uniforms were shades of pink and grey to coordinate with the décor. The tables and chairs were Canadian-made, the chairs upholstered with a material called Fabrikoid.

In planning the Montreal foyer, to be used occasionally as a tea room or lounge, Carlu opted for function over form, so that chairs, armchairs and couches were of "very simple design." The upholstery was "mouse grey, black and pink — harmonizing with the black satinwood of the frame . . . The tea tables have clear glass tops resting on blades of Monel metal" (*The Architectural Record*, Volume 69, #6, June, 1931).

Ostrich Fans and Diamond Tiaras

Lady Eaton with her niece Isobel was received by King George v and Queen Mary in the early 1930s. The invitation to attend court, which came from the Lord Chamberlain, directed gentlemen to wear their medals and women to wear evening attire, including their feathers. Lady Eaton chose a pink gown, shaded to deep rose, and a heavily beaded pink-and-rose velvet train, accessorized by her pink ostrich fan and her diamond tiara and feathers. The two women later reported on the occasion to a Toronto meeting of the Eaton's Girl's Club. They modelled their gowns, demonstrated their curtsies and answered questions about courtly procedure, including how Lord Chamberlain exited walking backward, so as not to turn his back on the monarchs.

Reception for returning service men and women,
Eaton Hall, September 12, 1946

Eaton's saw participation in the celebration of important events in the Dominion of Canada as a responsibility to its customers. When George VI was crowned in 1936, Eaton's stores across the country were decorated for the occasion, and the Toronto flagship store was decked in banners and bunting, with a spectacular decoration over the main doors acknowledging the coronation. At a ceremonial dinner in Ottawa, a golden bowl specially made in one of Eaton's factories was presented to the King and Queen.

Lady Eaton was also presented at the court of George VI with her future daughter-in-law Signy Steffason, a 20-year-old Icelandic beauty from Winnipeg. On June 23, 1935, Lady Eaton held an engagement party in the gardens at Ardwold for her son, John David, and his fiancée. Two thousand guests roamed Ardwold's expansive lawns, lingered in the late June afternoon by the big pool and fountain, and walked by the formal rose gardens and the ivy-covered pergola. Refreshments were served in a large marquee, vivid with pink peonies, on the north side of the house, and entertainment was provided by the Irish Regiment Band and Pipers. For the occasion, Signy Steffason wore a dress of *broderie anglaise* with puffed sleeves and a velvet waistband and a wide-brimmed brown straw hat. Lady Eaton wore a gauzy frock of white organdy sprigged with small blue flowers, a shoulder cape and a blue straw hat with an eyelet-embroidered edge.

Queen Street store decorated for coronation of King George VI and Queen Elizabeth: "Long may they reign"

Signy and John David married at Kawandag, the Eaton Muskoka summer estate, on August 9, 1935. Subsequently, the family's social focus shifted to Eaton Hall, the 670-acre farm and family estate north of Toronto near King City. Sir Henry Pellatt, who built Casa Loma and was the Eaton's neighbour at Ardwold, had recommended the

King Township property to them. It was Sir John's intention to retire there, and during his lifetime his family often visited their country retreat, picnicking and fishing on the grounds, using the existing farmhouse as a base. When Lady Eaton returned to Canada permanently, she decided to move the family to the farm in King Township, and to leave Ardwold forever.

Construction on Eaton Hall began in 1937. The turreted 35-room building, designed in a style adapted from a 16th-century Norman château, was built of Humber Valley stone and crowned with red roof tiles. While Eaton Hall was being built, Ardwold was dynamited, and the 11-acre plot on which it stood was divided into lots for a new housing project. The new Eaton estate, with residential quarters at Eaton Hall and the Villa Fiori, the original farmhouse, became Lady Eaton's home. The Eaton family was expanding, as two of Lady Eaton's sons had already married. "It was a foregone conclusion," she mused, "that the house had to be big . . . I was determined that Eaton Hall would be ample enough for any and all family gatherings in future years" (*Memory's Wall*, page 174).

The Great Hall on the main floor stretched between Eaton Hall's two wings. One wing housed the music room and the library, while the other contained the kitchens, flower room and the formal dining room, decorated in Louis XV period style. Lady Eaton used a smaller dining room upstairs, furnished in French provincial style, with toile wallpaper. Her private apartment included a bedroom, sunroom and large sitting room with a satinwood grand piano, one of four pianos in the house. The ground floor of Eaton Hall, with its ballroom and sport rooms, could accommodate employees from an entire department.

Lady Eaton loved a party, and presided over Eaton's functions as part of her ongoing involvement with the human side of the store. Scores of staff parties took place at the farm north of Toronto, for bakery staff, kitchen workers, caretakers, managers and dietitians. Employees were happy to be invited, as "out at the farm there was everything to do, and delicious and substantial 'eats' from the appetizing salads and cold meats to ice cream and punch" (*Flash*, *1937*).

Lady Eaton returned to court in 1937 to present her daughters Florence Mary and Evlyn Beatrice to the British monarchs. When her daughter was married in 1940, the reception for Florence Mary and Frank McEachern was held at Eaton Hall. The bride and groom arrived at the King Township estate in Ladybird, Lady Eaton's beloved 1912 Rolls Royce limousine.

A dinner was given in Lady Eaton's honour at the Round Room on December 16, 1941, to acknowledge the 20th anniversary of her election to the Board of Directors. A celebratory affair, the evening included a speech by the guest of honour. Lady Eaton recalled accepting a position on the Board with the proviso that she was not to be given special consideration because she was a woman. "I know that if my ideas are not sound they will be scrapped, and if they are sound they will be given consideration."

The menu featured chilled half lobster, consommé with mushrooms, roast young duckling with orange sauce, creamed cauliflower, candied sweet potatoes, cold asparagus vinaigrette, hot mince tarts and demitasse.

Lady Eaton retired from Eaton's Board of Directors two years later, on February 23, 1943, having remained a director until just after her son John David assumed the presidency. She was very proud to have worked with Eaton's four presidents —Timothy Eaton, her husband, his cousin R.Y. Eaton, and her eldest son.

However, though Lady Eaton may not have been heavily involved in the store management, she did take an active role in the Eaton's assistance to the war effort. During those years, Lady Eaton made her home a sanctuary, supporting seven English children and two mothers at Eaton Hall, and offering it as a convalescent home for members of the Royal Canadian Navy.

Lady Eaton also headed the campaign to build Sunnybrook Hospital, a dedicated facility for military personnel and veterans. She took part in demonstrations, and even donned a sandwich board during a downtown Toronto demonstration in support of building Sunnybrook to replace the inadequate hospital at Christie Pits.

Following the war, Eaton's staged welcome-home events for returning employees who had seen active duty. The company presented them with gold signet rings at a series of dinners and events in Toronto, Montreal, Moncton, Winnipeg and Calgary. Lady Eaton presided at these events. In Montreal, the welcome-home dinner took place at Le 9e. Lady Eaton began her speech by saying she hoped she could make the group understand the sympathy extended to them by the Eaton family, both the "Big Family" and the small one.

John David Eaton hosted 1,700 veterans at Eaton Hall on Thursday, September 12, 1946. Military bands played, Lady Eaton and John David Eaton made speeches, signet rings and war service badges were awarded to the veterans, and bountiful food and drink were served at an outdoor supper under the marquee.

While visiting London in 1949, Lady Eaton had an hour-long audience with Queen Mary at Marlborough House. Lady Eaton was chair of the executive committee of the United Empire Fund for Britain, and had sent members of the royal family samples of the standard food packages that the organization distributed in Britain following the war, containing turkey, ham, butter, sugar and pie. Impressed with this relief effort for the British population, the Queen wished to speak privately with Lady Eaton, who observed that the monarch was a woman of great calm, with a glowing, spirited quality.

'Tis the Season

In addition to elegant events at the Eaton estates and on store premises, the company was known for its annual Christmas festivities, windows and parades. Generations of small children thronged to visit Eaton's Christmas windows, or craved an "Eaton's Beauty Doll," annually imported from Germany (first advertised in a 1900 catalogue for $1), and its Christmas Wish Book was inspiration for many happy hours of daydreaming. Hundreds of carol sheets were sent to hospitals and schools each year, and provided to customers in the stores for evenings of carol singing.

The first Toyland in an Eaton's store had celebrated the birth of Sir John and Lady Eaton's first child, Timothy Craig, in 1903. The first Eaton's Santa Claus parades had been held in Winnipeg and

Santa with children in Centennial plaid clothing, 1967

CHRISTMAS CAROLS

PRESENTED WITH THE COMPLIMENTS OF EATON'S

1

AWAY IN A MANGER

Away in a manger,
No crib for a bed,
The little Lord Jesus
Laid down His sweet head.
The stars in the bright sky
Looked down where He lay,
The little Lord Jesus
Asleep on the hay.

The cattle are lowing,
The Baby awakes,
But little Lord Jesus
No crying He makes.
I love Thee, Lord Jesus;
Look down from the sky,
And stay by my side
Until morning is nigh.

Be near me, Lord Jesus,
I ask Thee to stay
Close by me for ever,
And love me, I pray.
Bless all the dear children
In Thy tender care,
And fit us for heaven
To live with Thee there.

2

WHILE SHEPHERDS WATCHED

While shepherds watched their flocks by night,
All seated on the ground,
The Angel of the Lord came down,
And glory shone around.
"Fear not," said he (for mighty dread
Had seized their troubled minds);
"Glad tidings of great joy I bring
To you and all mankind.

"To you in David's town this day
Is born of David's line
A Saviour, who is Christ the Lord;
And this shall be the sign:
The heavenly Babe you there shall find
To human view displayed,
All meanly wrapped in swathing bands,
And in a manger laid."

Thus spake the Seraph: and forthwith
Appeared a shining throng
Of angels praising God, who thus
Addressed their joyful song:
"All glory be to God on high,
And to the earth be peace:
Good-will henceforth from heaven to men
Begin and never cease."

3

O COME, ALL YE FAITHFUL

O come, all ye faithful,
Joyful and triumphant,
O come ye, O come ye to Bethlehem;
Come and behold Him
Born, the King of angels;
O come, let us adore Him, Christ the Lord.

God of God,
Light of Light,
Lo! He abhors not the Virgin's womb;
Very God,
Begotten, not created;
O come, let us adore Him, Christ the Lord.

Sing, choirs of angels,
Sing in exultation,
Sing, all ye citizens of heaven above:
"Glory to God
In the highest";
O come, let us adore Him, Christ the Lord.

Yea, Lord, we greet Thee,
Born this happy morning;
Jesus, to Thee be glory given;
Word of the Father,
Now in flesh appearing;
O come, let us adore Him, Christ the Lord.

Extra copies of these Carol Sheets may be obtained on request from The T. Eaton Co. Limited.

Christmas carols sheet, c. 1950

Toronto in 1905. Believed to be the first such events in the world, the parades quickly became a Canadian tradition.

A small affair at first, the Toronto parade featured Santa arriving in a wagon drawn by one horse, sitting on top of a huge packing crate. In 1909, the parade was a miniature representation of Admiral Peary's fabled expedition to the North Pole. Jack Eaton delighted in riding at the head of the parade in one of his treasured cars. He was also rumoured to have made an incognito appearance as Santa in one of the parades. In 1913, live reindeer pulled Santa's sleigh. They were brought by government steamer from Labrador to Quebec City, and from there shipped to Toronto by train. After the parade they were given to a farm in northern Ontario. From 1913 to 1915, the Toronto parade was followed by a pageant at Toronto's Massey Hall.

Not only did the audiences of 9,000 children and parents — there were three receptions in the day — shout and clap their hands, but all the Nursery Rhymes and pages and fairies and other storybook folk were there on the platform to greet Santa with songs and dances and a whole lot of beautiful things which made you think you were at a real old London Pantomime. For

Christmas parade pageant, Massey Hall, November 1913

Punkinhead c. 1950

which the Eaton staff were wholly responsible — for music, costumes, scenery and "libretto." Since 1916, when Toyland took up its Christmas quarters on the spacious main floor of the Furniture Building, all festivities following the great Arrival have been featured there — Punch and Judy Shows in real old-time English fashion, Marionettes such as you seldom see outside of France, and Santa Claus himself in the midst of it all to shake hands with the children, and hear what they have to say about how good they have been, what they want etc.; though if the truth be told, it must be related that many a kiddy who has rehearsed his speech many times in dream and reality, finally reaches the old gentleman tongue-tied. (Golden Jubilee, pages 218, 220*)*

The Eaton's Santa Claus parade required a dozen staff working full-time organizing, building floats, making costumes and papier mâché headdresses. Jim Brockie, head of Eaton's public relations, oversaw the parade for 35 years. Every year, along with other parade workers, he walked the five miles of the parade route to glimpse the delight on the faces of onlooking children.

The parade took place first in Montreal, then the floats and costumes were shipped to Toronto. The parades occurred in November, before the snow fell. For many watchers, the parades were associated with the beginning of the Christmas shopping season. Each year, following the parade, Santa went straight to Eaton's to open Toyland and begin his personal visits with young children.

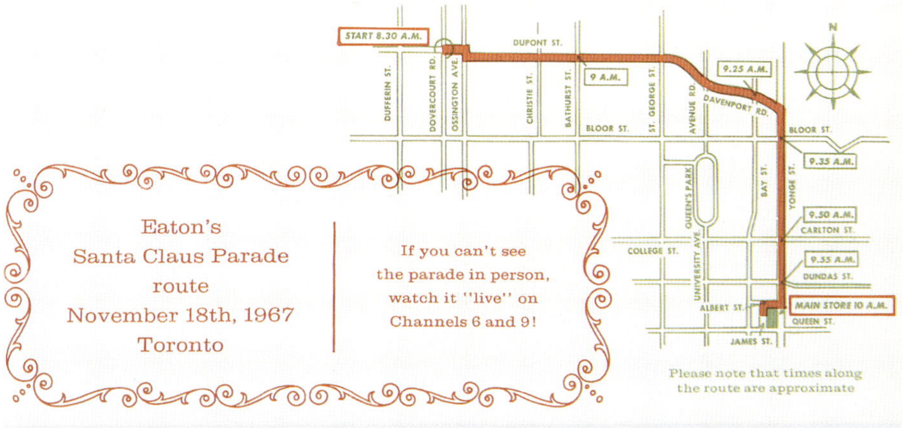

Toronto parade route card, 1967

Soon, the parade was reported to be a mile long, with scores of vividly decorated floats, more than a dozen marching bands, and more than 1,000 costumed paraders who each paid a small sum and were rewarded with hot chocolate, cookies and doughnuts at the end of the parade route.

Favourite parade characters included Cinderella, Gulliver, Little Bo-Peep, Sleeping Beauty and other fairy-tale figures, but no Eaton's Christmas parade was complete without Punkinhead, who was introduced in 1948 as a store mascot. For several years, a special Punkinhead storybook was produced by Eaton's at Christmas. The little bear with the tousled topknot appeared on everything from collector's plates to special Christmas cookies to children's merchandise, including toys, watches, pyjamas, mittens and hats. The plush toy Punkinhead was manufactured for Eaton's for almost a decade by Merrythought Toy Company.

At the conclusion of each parade came Santa, discreetly followed by a car with darkened windows, which carried a doctor and nurse in case of Santa mishaps (one year his pants fell down!). Also in the car

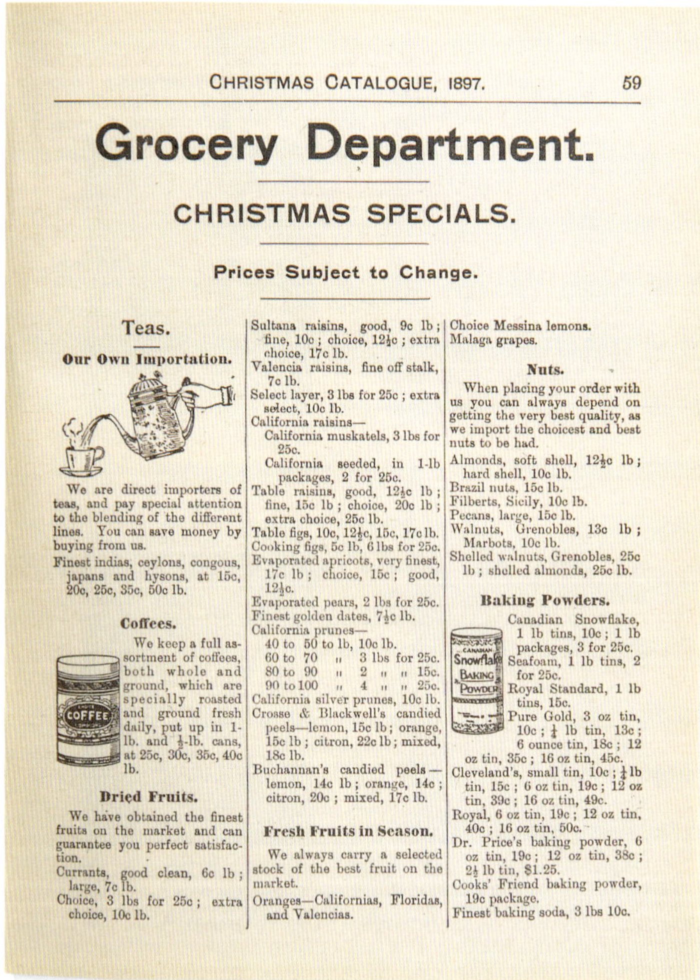

CHRISTMAS CATALOGUE, 1897. 59

Grocery Department.

CHRISTMAS SPECIALS.

Prices Subject to Change.

Teas.

Our Own Importation.

We are direct importers of teas, and pay special attention to the blending of the different lines. You can save money by buying from us.

Finest indias, ceylons, congous, japans and hysons, at 15c, 20c, 25c, 35c, 50c lb.

Coffees.

We keep a full assortment of coffees, both whole and ground, which are specially roasted and ground fresh daily, put up in 1-lb. and ½-lb. cans, at 25c, 30c, 35c, 40c lb.

Dried Fruits.

We have obtained the finest fruits on the market and can guarantee you perfect satisfaction.

Currants, good clean, 6c lb; large, 7c lb.

Choice, 3 lbs for 25c; extra choice, 10c lb.

Sultana raisins, good, 9c lb; fine, 10c; choice, 12½c; extra choice, 17c lb.

Valencia raisins, fine off stalk, 7c lb.

Select layer, 3 lbs for 25c; extra select, 10c lb.

California raisins—

California muskatels, 3 lbs for 25c.

California seeded, in 1-lb packages, 2 for 25c.

Table raisins, good, 12½c lb; fine, 15c lb; choice, 20c lb; extra choice, 25c lb.

Table figs, 10c, 12½c, 15c, 17c lb.

Cooking figs, 5c lb, 6 lbs for 25c.

Evaporated apricots, very finest, 17c lb; choice, 15c; good, 12½c.

Evaporated pears, 2 lbs for 25c.

Finest golden dates, 7½c lb.

California prunes—

40 to 50 to lb, 10c lb.

60 to 70 " 3 lbs for 25c.

80 to 90 " 2 " " 15c.

90 to 100 " 4 " " 25c.

California silver prunes, 10c lb.

Crosse & Blackwell's candied peels—lemon, 15c lb; orange, 15c lb; citron, 22c lb; mixed, 18c lb.

Buchannan's candied peels—lemon, 14c lb; orange, 14c; citron, 20c; mixed, 17c lb.

Fresh Fruits in Season.

We always carry a selected stock of the best fruit on the market.

Oranges—Californias, Floridas, and Valencias.

Choice Messina lemons.

Malaga grapes.

Nuts.

When placing your order with us you can always depend on getting the very best quality, as we import the choicest and best nuts to be had.

Almonds, soft shell, 12½c lb; hard shell, 10c lb.

Brazil nuts, 15c lb.

Filberts, Sicily, 10c lb.

Pecans, large, 15c lb.

Walnuts, Grenobles, 13c lb; Marbots, 10c lb.

Shelled walnuts, Grenobles, 25c lb; shelled almonds, 25c lb.

Baking Powders.

Canadian Snowflake, 1 lb tins, 10c; 1 lb packages, 3 for 25c.

Seafoam, 1 lb tins, 2 for 25c.

Royal Standard, 1 lb tins, 15c.

Pure Gold, 3 oz tin, 10c; ¼ lb tin, 13c; 6 ounce tin, 18c; 12 oz tin, 35c; 16 oz tin, 45c.

Cleveland's, small tin, 10c; ¼ lb tin, 15c; 6 oz tin, 19c; 12 oz tin, 39c; 16 oz tin, 49c.

Royal, 6 oz tin, 19c; 12 oz tin, 40c; 16 oz tin, 50c.

Dr. Price's baking powder, 6 oz tin, 19c; 12 oz tin, 38c; 2½ lb tin, $1.25.

Cooks' Friend baking powder, 19c package.

Finest baking soda, 3 lbs 10c.

Christmas specials, 1897 catalogue

was a fully dressed and bearded "spare" Santa, in case of a more serious emergency.

During and after World War II, Eaton's also hosted annual Christmas parties for the children of employees active in the services. Lady Eaton attended and talked proudly about the fathers abroad and the Eaton's Employees War Auxiliary.

The preparation of baked goods for Christmas began in September in Toronto, with the making of Christmas cakes and shortbread in

the eighth floor Georgian Room kitchens. The Toronto employees magazine reported that the "most popular product, according to tonnage sold (we said tonnage and we mean tonnage, believe us) is the rich, dark fruitcake, which sells in twice and a half the quantity of its nearest rivals, the light fruitcake and plum pudding. Next come the attractive little shortbreads and cookies, with mincemeat — even in fourth position — disappearing to the tune of some two tons at Christmastime" (*Flash*, 1950).

Punkinhead cookies were ginger-and-sugar cookies cut to represent the little tousle-headed bear. Shortbreads were offered in various festive season shapes — holly and bells, Christmas trees and stockings. Light and dark fruitcake was available by mail order. The Toronto kitchens prepared about six tons of cake each year, packing individual orders in distinctive red-and-silver containers.

Christmas pins: Season's Greetings; Breakfast with Santa

Eaton's employees attended an annual Christmas luncheon and supper at which they consumed mountains of festive food. *Flash,* Eaton's employee newsletter, reported that for one day's annual treats, employees' kitchens prepared 2½ tons of turkey, 1,900 pounds of potatoes, 65 gallons of gravy, 50 cases of peas, 200 pounds of apple jelly, 400-dozen rolls, 140 gallons of milk, 100 gallons of coffee and 90 gallons of tea. The annual meal remained affordable; an ad for the Employees' Turkey Dinner in 1955 offered turkey and all the trimmings for 55¢.

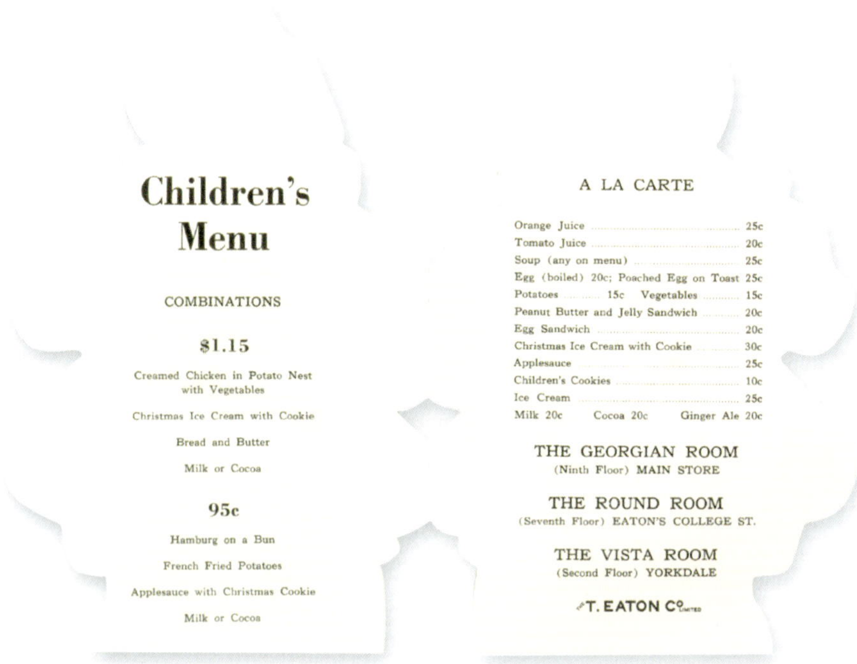

Children's Menu

COMBINATIONS

$1.15

Creamed Chicken in Potato Nest with Vegetables

Christmas Ice Cream with Cookie

Bread and Butter

Milk or Cocoa

95c

Hamburg on a Bun

French Fried Potatoes

Applesauce with Christmas Cookie

Milk or Cocoa

A LA CARTE

Orange Juice ... 25c
Tomato Juice ... 20c
Soup (any on menu) ... 25c
Egg (boiled) 20c; Poached Egg on Toast 25c
Potatoes ... 15c Vegetables ... 15c
Peanut Butter and Jelly Sandwich ... 20c
Egg Sandwich ... 20c
Christmas Ice Cream with Cookie ... 30c
Applesauce ... 25c
Children's Cookies ... 10c
Ice Cream ... 25c
Milk 20c Cocoa 20c Ginger Ale 20c

THE GEORGIAN ROOM
(Ninth Floor) MAIN STORE

THE ROUND ROOM
(Seventh Floor) EATON'S COLLEGE ST.

THE VISTA ROOM
(Second Floor) YORKDALE

T. EATON Co LIMITED

Children's Christmas menu, inscribed "all d.r. Toronto — used Dec. '65"

Christmas was a busy season in the restaurants, with sold-out breakfast visits from Santa, luncheon dates, grandparents' treats and harried shoppers pausing for a meal or a snack. In the last week before Christmas, the restaurants became quiet again, as shoppers reached a pitch of activity and were too busy to stop for lunch.

Breakfast with Santa was a popular custom in Eaton's dining rooms right across the country. Special-occasion meals and treats for children, such as those offered on the Christmas menus, were very different from present-day party food for young people. A menu in the shape of Punkinhead offered children's fare; others were in the shape of Santa, carousels or clowns. Menus for children were simple and emphatically pre-junk-food — not a pizza or chicken nugget in sight! Children ate what grown-ups ate, in smaller portions. They

Children's clown menu cover, 1940s, used in the Round Room and Georgian Room

were served in the dining rooms on special china that was black, off-white and fawn and decorated with nursery rhyme figures.

Ice cream was a favourite seasonal treat with Christmas baking. A rectangular silver tray of sauces accompanied the ice cream, which was served in small silver bowls. Children helped themselves to butterscotch, marshmallow, strawberry and chocolate sauce. A clown with a face made of a small scoop of vanilla ice cream, a hat made of an inverted cone, cookie ears, a maraschino cherry slice for a mouth, and chocolate-chip eyes was a special treat generations of children recall with affection.

Lady Eaton maintained Eaton Hall as the gathering place for annual Christmas dinners and festivities. For many years, she hosted a

Christmas Suggestions flyer, Georgian Room cake counters

candlelit evening carol service for the King City community in the Great Hall. The family's crèche, with figures collected during the family's years in Europe, a communion table, and a Michelangelo cherub from Florence decorated the hall. After carol singing and communion, the company adjourned to the ballroom for turkey, ham, spiced beef, Christmas cake, mince tarts, coffee and punch.

Eaton Hall was the site of many annual Christmas company events as well. The Hunt ballroom was decorated with swags of dark green cedar and illuminated by Christmas-tree lights and clusters of ornaments. Queen Mary's personal Christmas card to Lady Eaton always stood on the mantel. Buffet tables extended the length of the room, boasting huge silver bowls of deep scarlet carnations.

On Christmas Day, it was Lady Eaton's tradition to host the family's dinner. In the late afternoon the Eatons assembled by the

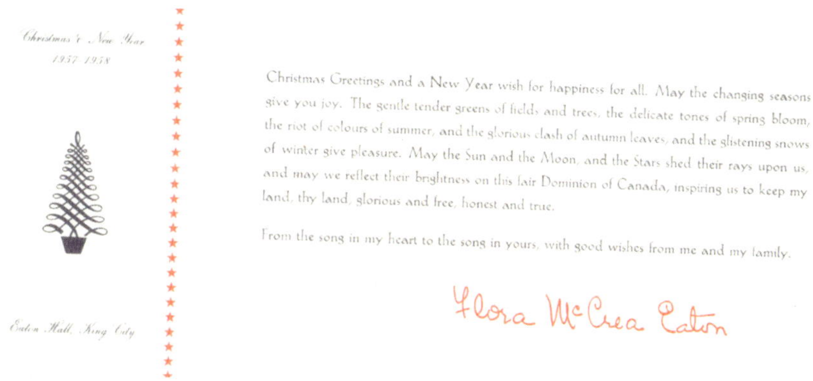

Christmas & New Year
1957 1958

Eaton Hall, King City

Christmas Greetings and a New Year wish for happiness for all. May the changing seasons give you joy. The gentle tender greens of fields and trees, the delicate tones of spring bloom, the riot of colours of summer, and the glorious clash of autumn leaves, and the glistening snows of winter give pleasure. May the Sun and the Moon, and the Stars shed their rays upon us, and may we reflect their brightness on this fair Dominion of Canada, inspiring us to keep my land, thy land, glorious and free, honest and true.

From the song in my heart to the song in yours, with good wishes from me and my family.

Flora McCrea Eaton

Lady Eaton's Christmas and New Year card, 1957–58

Christmas tree at Eaton Hall. Oysters on the half shell were served with thin bread and butter and Rhine wine. Santa arrived to present gifts, the children were entertained with magic tricks, and then the family went in to Christmas dinner. Lady Eaton sat with the youngest members of the family at the head table, making them the VIPs for the day. When dinner was served, each child at the table was given a drumstick to ensure that fairness reigned and they were kept fully occupied.

It was Lady Eaton's custom each year to write Christmas cards to her many friends and business associates. Signed in her square, balanced hand, they extended her warm greetings and her hopes for peace and prosperity.

Have You Tested the Butterscotch Filling Lately?

During the war, it was essential that dietitians learn to cope with shortages and cook with ingredients that were available in a time of rationing. Wartime records from the Queen Street store indicate that quantities of butter and sugar were checked daily. Dairy products, particularly butter and cream, continued to be staples of the restaurants and kitchens, as they had been since the early days of ice cream and oyster stew. The fat content of fresh bran muffins, salad dressings with a whipping cream base, coffee with 24 percent cream, cakes baked with pounds of butter, and cream sauces was lowered, as part of a general trend toward lighter fare and conservation of supplies.

Waitresses at the warming cupboards in the Georgian Room kitchen, 1945, from a Globe and Mail *series entitled* "The Eaton's You'll Never See"

Winnipeg's Grill Room, c. 1940

Fresh produce was in short supply, however, which made menu-planning a nightmare. Dietitians' notes from the period contain many references to supplementary items when produce was unavailable. Standard offerings, such as Georgian Room salad plates, were altered by the shortages. "On June 1st, the fruit salad situation is the most serious it has ever been, with no pineapple, bananas, apples, dates, figs or nuts (beyond a very few). Even though package gelatine is very expensive and my cost for gelatine alone, two thirds of 1¢ per mould, it seems advisable to use it, as thus we can obtain both variety and colour . . ." (Violet Ryley, June 1, 1942).

The Georgian Room, 1939–40

Spurred by the need to be organized to deal with these less than ideal circumstances, Eaton's began training dietetic interns in 1942. Under the guiding eye of Violet Ryley, a three-month summer apprenticeship and a 10-month internship in "Administrative Dietetics" provided courses in food preparation, administration, merchandising, purchasing, storeroom control, dining room, cafeteria and luncheonette matters, bookkeeping, ice cream manufacture, the personnel office and job analysis. Trainees were put to work in a staff cafeteria called the Beanery, in the butcher shop and in the bakeries, acquiring practical experience in all aspects of food production and service.

From the Desk of V.M. Ryley

If I were Lady E. what would I want?

Thoughtfulness

Kindness

Charm

Courtesy

Efficiency

Therefore, make a study of efficiency.

What can you do in quantity?

Cream sauces

Mayonnaise

Applesauce

Dozens of things . . .

The dietitians and production staff, including the interns, held formal "tastings" every day at 11 a.m. Eaton's offered students in the program $22 per week and two meals a day. Student dietitians were expected to arrive for work in the morning wearing black dresses, hats and gloves to distinguish them from waitresses in the dining rooms. (One dietitian recalled her horror upon realizing that she was wearing the same dress as Lady Eaton!) Students were provided with at least eight outfits, but these were laundered by the company. Each intern also received a $15 book allowance to keep up with publications in the developing field of commercial dietetics.

A small pamphlet entitled *Notes on How to Obtain Quality in Food*, published by the company, offers some insight into the meticulous attention to planning, food handling and preparation that was at the core of the dietitians' training. Recipes were handwritten by the dietitians with scrupulous care. Ryley's influence and standards of presentation are visible on every page.

One of the twelve principles of efficiency is to clearly define your goal. In all food work, this goal is perfection in quality and appearance for this particular food. The secret of success in food work is perfection of detail. By this I mean:

1. *Flavour:* the difference between a $50-a-month cook and a $500-a-month expert is often a fine discrimination in flavour. Every cook should train himself so that he is an expert critic on flavour, and knows exactly whether the thing has too much or too little salt, or the required amount of lemon juice exactly the right flavour for that particular thing: for example, what is more tragic than to get a lovely fine chicken soup with a strong celery flavour predominating, or to get a poultry dressing reeking with seasoning, instead of delicately blended, or to get coffee which is just so-so, instead of being blended with the care that you would use in measuring the ingredients for a cake? Flavour is altogether the result of accurate measuring, care and discrimination, with strong emphasis on the accuracy of measurements . . .

2. *Texture:* the cook should test for texture. See if a soup or sauce is too thick, or too thin, or lumpy. Consider the texture; have it absolutely perfect for that particular food. If a cake, is it fine and moist; if a jelly, is it stiff or tender, etc.?

3. *Temperature:* temperature is so vital that it is given third place. The best food in the world can be ruined if served at the wrong

temperature. A steak partially cooled is ruined. Anything that is supposed to be served sizzling hot, should be sizzling hot or it is not right, or if supposed to be icy cold, it should be icy cold.

4. *Colour:* what is worse than food that is the wrong colour? A tenderloin steak can be absolutely ruined if carelessly cooked and a sad grey colour. It should be browned to exactly the right shade. Toast is judged almost entirely by its golden brown colour; if burnt, it is unattractive, or if too pale, no person wants it. This question of colour may be just the difference between a first-class success and a complete failure. Everything cooked by either frying, pan-broiling or clear-fire-broiling depends for its ultimate success upon colour.

5. *General Appearance (Size, shape, regularity, etc.):* general appearance means so much: for example, the same ingredients may be cut in great coarse chunks and made into a stew that is most unpalatable, or beautifully diced and the same food is a success.

6. *Arrangement and Colour Scheme:* more good food is ruined in the serving than possibly in any other place, for example, a vegetable plate owes its attractiveness almost entirely to colour scheme and arrangement. It can be either a work of art or an awful hodge-podge. This also holds good for all such foods as salads and desserts.

(*Notes on How to Obtain Quality in Food*)

Daily tasting became a foundation of quality control in the Eaton's production kitchens. *Notes on How to Obtain Quality in Food* puts forward the virtues of tasting, offering a few tips:

Each cook or salad worker should learn how to taste correctly: have a teaspoon of your own, and wash it carefully every time it is used. Always observe the following points when tasting:

1. Concentrate — do not let your mind waver while tasting.

2. Taste rapidly.

3. Always use your imagination. Can you imagine anything that would taste better than what you are tasting now, and if so, what would make this difference? Consult the person in charge and find out if it is something that would involve a great deal of expense, as usually the thing required is something both simple and inexpensive.

One dietitian with a great fondness for butterscotch tart filling had a like-minded friend in the kitchens. "Have you tested the butter scotch filling lately?" they asked every time they saw one another, and dutifully checked every half hour to make sure that it was still up to standard. Eaton's test kitchens were happy spots for the taster, as products were tasted, tested and chosen with great attention to detail. Grocery departments, the Hostess Shops and Eaton's candy departments benefited from these efforts at quality control; the candy department's taste panels were particularly popular.

Many of the test kitchens' findings are signed by F.J. Hall. Miss Hall was a long-time Eaton's dietitian, a university graduate who had been hired during the Depression as a Georgian Room hostess at a salary of $12 a week. She had a reputation among her colleagues and students for having a sense of taste so keen that she could distinguish any spice or flavouring in any recipe.

As the store continued to add new locations and food services, the use of "cycle menus" was introduced. Menus developed for spring, summer, fall and winter came into rotation on a national basis. Before the introduction of cycle menus, dietitians in each restaurant developed menus independently, though there was constant testing and comparison of products, as well as exchanges of recipes and prepared dishes among the restaurants.

Seasonal themes and holidays such as Christmas, Easter, St. Patrick's Day and Lent were featured in menu planning. The production of new menus each day represented an immense task for dietitians and office staff. Daily menus were typed, corrected and adjusted, then typed again. Although the kitchens made extensive use of frozen foods, the menus are a reminder that the availability of fresh fruits and vegetables was often limited and specific to a few weeks of the year. This idea of using seasonal, local produce has again come into vogue in recent years.

The dietitians' training encouraged them to plan two weeks in advance, then revise and finalize their menus before scheduling the kitchen staff's work plans. Dietitians were encouraged to keep their ideas current, to overcome personal dislikes and to cultivate their curiosity about new foods. They were directed to present a clear description of each food item on their menus and to "avoid foreign terms."

Friction was the main cause of staff turnover, so dietitians were urged by their supervisors to be honest in their self-appraisal, and to be intelligent, logical and compassionate while maintaining authority and cultivating their skills in delegating and organizing others' time. Food science it was, but some of the dietitians also recall their work as a career in applied psychology.

Some of the kitchen work was done during the early shift by "night men," including bakers and butchers. During the day, a complex network of bakery workers, preparation staff, salad and sandwich makers, captains, waitresses, bus girls, fountain dispensers and food checkers worked in the kitchens, restaurants, snack bars and cafeterias. It was the dietitians' job to train, oversee, schedule and replace the staff when necessary. During the 1940s, only married women could be hired to work part time; full-time work went first to men.

Any person who keeps a work table cluttered and disorderly shows that he has a disorderly mind, and that person will neither attain speed nor system in the handling of work. Motion study is closely allied to order and system, and we all know what miracles are accomplished by conservation of movements.

Use of human body

1. Both hands stop & start together.

2. Both hands should not be idle at the same instant.

3. Motions of arms, simultaneous in opposite and symmetrical directions.

4. Use lowest body classification possible — i.e. finger movement, wrist & finger.

5. Momentum should be employed to assist worker wherever possible — reduced to minimum if it has to be overcome by muscular energy.

6. Curved lines of motion are preferable to abrupt changes of direction.

7. Ballistic movements faster, easier than controlled movements.

8. Rhythm essential to smooth and automatic operation.

(*Notes on How to Obtain Quality in Food*)

Toronto grocery packing, 1940s

During the war, Violet Ryley and Kathleen Jeffs, a protegé of Ryley's who went on to manage the Montreal store's restaurants for 23 years, were called upon by the armed services for training and information. Ryley was involved with the dietetics training for the military at the advisory level, while Jeffs spent the war years as Chief Messing Officer for the Royal Canadian Air Force. Wing Officer Jeffs was the first woman to organize food services for any of the armed forces, and received the Order of the British Empire for her services. After the war, the RCAF Chef's Training Course was run through Eaton's Administrative Dietetics Intern program until the mid-1950s.

Food preparation workers at special tables 26 inches high, which "eliminate fatigue and adds to the pleasure, attractiveness and effectiveness of their work," "The Eaton's You'll Never See"

Over the course of her 26 years with Eaton's, Ryley's influence helped raise standards of food and service in Eaton's restaurants all across Canada. "As far as advance in knowledge of food values, proper cooking and serving either in civilian or military service, Violet Ryley was always consulted, and few know the time she gave in an advisory capacity to make of food service a fine science" (Lady Eaton, 1952 speech to Bolton Rotary Club).

As part of company-wide plans for expansion after the war, Eaton's contemplated opening a Toronto catering service (a rival department store had started a successful one), but found the project too costly in terms of time and resources. Within the stores, however, the restaurants often catered dinners and parties, and patrons could order cakes and sandwiches from the cake counters to be carried home or delivered. Birthday cakes could be custom ordered and inscribed as requested. Delivery orders for cakes, cookies, pastry, cooked meats and fish, box lunches and sandwiches were packed in the boxing room and sent to the cake counters for pick-up.

A box lunch from the Georgian Room counter was an affordable treat. At a cost of about 50¢, each box contained mock chicken, potato salad, a butter tart and a roll, and were often bought by customers as take-out picnic food. Dietitians recall customers requesting "quiet fruit" when purchasing box lunches to take to the film *Gone with the Wind.* Photographs of Eaton's kitchen staff parties show

The Boxing Room, "The Eaton's You'll Never See"

scores of men and women picnicking at long tables on Toronto's Centre Island — each with a boxed lunch.

Even after the war ended, some effects of rationing lingered, and fresh produce and certain other foods were difficult to obtain. For example, Hamilton's Green Room didn't note the end of "meatless days" in the restaurant until August 16, 1947.

Pride in modern methods meant that Eaton's restaurants were always being upgraded. The Artofex, a Swiss-made mixer used in the bakeries, could mix about 400 pounds of dough per operation. It was used to make bread, bun and pastry dough, as well as Christmas puddings and mincemeat. Eaton's College Street store had a small bakery, which supplied the Round Room cake counter with muffins, tea biscuits, pies, cakes and cookies, while yeast products were brought in from the Queen Street bakery farther south along Yonge Street. The Montreal store's bakery supplied Le 9e, as well as making products for the main floor Blue Cake Counter.

Regardless of the menu item, Eaton's was ever vigilante in an effort to meet the "goodness of home cooking" standard:

Georgian Room cake counters Box Lunches cover, 1940s

Our objective is to have food come out of the oven or refrigerator at the moment it is needed — an extremely easy thing to say, but so difficult to accomplish. We want to serve fresh cookies which have been baked only an hour or so before serving; fruit pie that is still warm; crisp cooked vegetables which have just finished boiling, steaming, or baking and are served as quickly as one would at home. Since the highly undesirable process of aging begins almost as the food comes from the oven, steamer, or kettle, let us aim to serve that food before it becomes a moment older. We have much to live up to when patrons and customers compare our food with home-cooked meals — and they all do it! (Helen Buik, Manager of the Georgian Room, 1957*)*

Eaton's kitchens and bakeries had two levels of ingredients and expense. The Georgian Room, the Round Room, Le 9e, Hamilton's Green Room and Winnipeg's Grill Room were the Upper Floors. Cafeterias and lunchrooms were known as the Lower Floors, and had their own recipes and menus. Dietitians referred to recipes as "cheap" or "expensive." Their expensive recipes were reserved for serving in

Kitchen worker with an Artofex, "The Eaton's You'll Never See"

Upper Floor dining rooms, while the cheap recipes were prepared for the less formal restaurants. Essentially different versions of the same foods, cheap recipes used less butter and cream in baked goods, or substituted other ingredients. Products and recipes from various locations were constantly compared.

Dietitians learned to document all aspects of their work, from hygiene to the decimal points of costing cheap and expensive recipes. They were trained to see their work in an executive capacity, encompassing the delivery of quality food and the management of staff, facilities and resources. They also added a healthy dose of patriotism to everything they did.

The Georgian Room strives to serve Canadian food and features typically Canadian items on its menus. We do not use foreign phrases on our menu where there is an English equivalent.

French food is famous, but we feel Canadian food can be just as good, with the use of a little imagination in its preparation and selection. . . Maintaining the standards set up by Violet Ryley and Lady Eaton is a job we all work hard at. (A May, 1960 speech to Eaton's Women's Council, possibly written by dietitian Helen Buik)

The salad plate continued to be a feature of Eaton's lunchtime menus, served from the opening of the Georgian Room. Each day's salad contained from 14 to 17 ingredients, requiring melon-ballers, wafflers and other cutting devices to create variation in ingredients' texture and shape. One dietitian's sample salad recipe called for lettuce, watercress, a base of whipped cream with fruit, apple wedges, a cantaloupe ball, orange slices, grapefruit sections, watermelon, a glazed prune, red fresh fruit jelly, green grapes, pineapple and avocado. It was topped with peach, almond and pineapple dressing, consisting of one-part boiled dressing, drained crushed pineapple and sliced, browned almonds. The salad was decorated with an orange twist and a pale green marshmallow bonbon. A protein garnish, such as cream cheese rolled in coconut, or a bar of cheddar cheese, was always part of the salad plate. To ensure freshness, salads were assembled on a long "ice tray" and stored on chilled china plates.

Some fruit salads were served with an avocado dressing, others in half a cantaloupe. For cantaloupe fruit salad, whipped cream with peach, pear, Turkish delight, coconut and nuts was combined with orange slices, grapefruit sections, watermelon wedges, a cantaloupe ball, two fresh strawberries, two fresh Bing cherries, a green marshmallow bonbon garnish, a grape jelly waffle, a cheese bar rolled in chopped nuts, a honey dew waffle, an orange twist, a cucumber twist, mint and lettuce. These ingredients were arranged in a hollowed cantaloupe and topped with lemon fruit dressing.

Salad making assumed a dance-like quality along the assembly line. The salads were "built" — a predecessor of "tall food" — in contrast to the flat salads generally served elsewhere at the time. The secret lemon chiffon dressing served with the salads contained equal parts 40 percent whipped cream and Georgian Room lemon pie filling. The Georgian Room menu lists the fruit salad at $1.25, while the cost to make them was about 36¢ per plate. Less elaborate fruit salads were made in the cafeterias at a cost of about 16¢ per plate or 18¢ a bowl.

Lunchtime vegetable salad plates were also a popular item. Each plate had three lettuce cups of potato salad, cottage cheese and cabbage salad. The cups were individually garnished with hard-boiled egg slices or wedges; a fruit garnish was always included. The Georgian Room produced these plates for 28¢ while the cafeterias' cheaper version cost 17¢. Garnishes might be cut with a waffler, a knife or a potato-baller. Variety in the salads' appearance was a primary consideration.

Training notes for salad makers stressed order, practice, efficiency, and attention to the principles of colour, flavour and textural contrast in the arrangement of the plate, as well as to the effect of garnishes. Salad makers were encouraged, once they had mastered the general principles of what instructors called "artistic salad assembly," to strive for speed.

Eaton's test kitchens maintained standards and worked on new techniques, testing new recipes for commercial use and increasing them from small to commercial-scale quantities. They tried out new products and compared Eaton's products from the restaurants, bakery counters, soda fountains, cafeterias and snack bars. Observations were carefully noted.

Canadian cuisine was defined by the availability of ingredients, developed to exploit a short growing season and prepare for long winters — preserves and relishes for winter, sumptuous fruit pies and salads for summer. Beef and pork predominated in the national diet, which created a tendency toward savoury, heavy dishes. Spices were still considered exotic — foods were seasoned with salt and pepper, Worcestershire sauce, possibly mustard. Garlic, turmeric, coriander, shallots, star anise and tarragon? Not yet.

Salad Assembly Line for One Worker

1. Using a straight line production, the salad worker first places three lettuce cups on each of five plates, keeping in mind what each cup will contain, since some will need to be firmer and larger than others. This allows use of one complete head of lettuce before starting a second.

2. Lettuce cups are padded with shredded lettuce, as needed. To keep them in proper position and to achieve height, they may be propped with bits of lettuce.

3. Using a scoop, worker fills the main lettuce cup on each plate, which now forms the basis of garnishes.

4. In a similar manner, the second and third cups are filled.

5. Plates are now ready for garnishes. Worker picks up five garnishes at a time, using both hands where possible.

6. Garnishes are placed on plate so that each item on the plate will show distinctly. Garnishes are placed to achieve upward line and to gain height. Most frequently, they are placed squarely on top of the filled lettuce cups. Special attention is paid to contrast in colour, flavour and texture of garnishes. Celery hearts, parsley, watercress and/or mint are the final garnishes.

7. The salad worker now places the five completed salads on a tray and "hustles" them into the refrigerator to remain until serving time.

A memo, dated May 12, 1952, suggests ongoing limitations in the availability of ingredients, along with the following inventive luncheon suggestions:

Mushroom Soufflé with Tomato or Shrimp Sauce
Vegetable Plate with Hot Devilled Egg
Broccoli on Toast with Cheese Sauce and Bacon
Onion stuffed with Baked Beans
Creamed Eggs and Mushrooms in Patty Shells or Timbale
Poached Egg on Ham Toast with Cheese Sauce
Orange Tuna on Noodles (creamed tuna with added orange and lemon juice and rind)
Sliced Ham and Asparagus Spears on Toast with Foamy Mayonnaise

The dietitians were not above humour when discussing Canadian cuisine. A spirited address about coleslaw given by Miss Martin, one of the dietetic instructors, to a class of interns made the following observations, managing to be at once both wry and moralistic about taste and waste: "You are too often served a garnish of 'cold slaughter' with your grilled meats and as an added treat, a side dish of 'cold slaughter' as a substitute vegetable, which you have usually to beg for. Imagination will have to be a tremendous factor in the enjoyment of this meal. How many of us, I wonder, find the coleslaw left on the

Spring Menu Suggestions — Highlighting the Easter Season, March 14, 1953

March 21st ushers in spring and we have until June 21st to consider suitable menu items for this season of the year. We'll want our menus to have a "light" fresh touch . . .

- Fresh Cucumbers — very welcome at this time of year
- Beet and Horseradish Jelly Ring filled with cucumber in Sour Cream Dressing
- Stuffed Cucumber Slice (hollowed out centre of cucumber filled with Minced Ham or Egg filling, and the cucumber sliced) — could be used as a protein garnish on a Salad Plate
- Lime Cucumber Jelly is particularly fresh-looking
- Tomatoes are more plentiful than during the winter, so are welcome on any menu
- Sliced Tomato and Roquefort Butter Sandwich
- Stuffed Tomato with Seafood and Avocado Salad would be so suitable and pretty in the Easter season
- Sliced Tomatoes in Celery Seed Dressing or Anchovy Dressing
- Cauliflower in Tomato Aspic should give a new touch to your salads (cook cauliflower head just until barely tender; drain; set cauliflower up in bowl; pour slightly thickened aspic over, chill, unmold; cut in wedges; serve with mayonnaise or Thousand Island Dressing)
- Frozen Chicken Salad is a refreshing item on an Upper Floor salad (chicken, pineapple, nuts, whipped cream and mayonnaise)

Another frozen salad is made of fruit and has been made in the Round Room (banana, apricot, pineapple and cherry)
• Grape and Lemon Cream Ribbon Jelly would certainly give a touch of Easter to any Salad — as would Grape Jelly Mold with a tiny pineapple ring in the bottom
• Stuffed Prune with yellow cream-cheese and violet petal would be "light" and "Eastery" looking

plate? It is better not to serve any salad than a poor salad" (Miss Martin, March 1950).

For many years, Eaton's dietitians, exclusively women, were a subculture of the company's larger corporate family. As such, they enjoyed a few privileges not afforded the paying customers. While clientele paid top dollar for baskets of freshly baked rolls and bran, corn, cheese, blueberry, banana and raisin muffins (served with any order over 40¢), Eaton's staff enjoyed reduced rates.

Managers could order a fruit bowl, toast and milk as a quick lunch for 50¢, or a more substantial meal at a subsidized price. Managers were primarily men, however, and in the flagship Toronto Queen Street store the manager's dining room remained a men's enclave. The Clipper Room, adjoining the Round Room, was the management's retreat in the College Street store. The Clipper Room's "3-in-1 Plate Luncheon" — juice, a sandwich and dessert — was on offer for 35¢, while a piece of pie cost 20¢. Ceremonies for graduates of the dietetics internship program took place in the Clipper Room, as did the annual Eaton Management Association Christmas party —

Villa Fiori, Eaton Hall letterhead

possibly the only occasions on which strong drink was served in any Eaton's restaurant in the country.

While Lady Eaton oversaw the program for dietitians at the store, she also took an active interest in her own kitchen at Eaton Hall. Lady Eaton had hired an Irish woman, known only as Maude, to be her cook and though she was competent, she was quite unfamiliar with the ways of Canadian cooking. Tensions built as she tried to suit Lady Eaton's tastes. When asked to make a pie from the rhubarb growing in Eaton Hall's garden, Maude peeled the rhubarb and served Lady Eaton a pallid dish topped with a decoration of fancy pastry leaves. Lady Eaton summoned Dorothy Brown, a recent graduate of Eaton's dietetic internship program, to take over.

In 1948, Lady Eaton was living at the Villa Fiori, the smaller house on the Eaton estate, as Eaton Hall was too large for her. When Dorothy Brown arrived, the staff consisted of Maude, her friend Helen, a maid, and Harris, the butler. Lady Eaton treated Miss Brown well, understanding that she was somewhat in awe of the Eaton lifestyle and nervous about unfamiliar customs. Miss Brown wrote home, "Despite the finger bowls and the asparagus that is served as first course and eaten with the fingers, I haven't made any real *faux pas* yet — that I'm aware of" (Dorothy Brown, May 8, 1948, letter from Eaton Hall farm).

One of the first dishes Dorothy Brown prepared at the Villa Fiori was a lemon soufflé. Unfortunately, Miss Brown's profile in the kitchen quickly became an issue with Maude, and the situation deteriorated. Miss Brown's letters reveal that the domestic politics were growing increasingly tense:

Lady Eaton went to the kitchen to tell her what a good soufflé she had made. Maude looked at her with a face like a meat ax, then asked how they were getting into the city on Thursday, their day off. "By bus," L.E. replied. "Well then I'm not going," says Maude . . . Friday morning I came down with the menus and Maude flew off about being treated like dirt. So after giving her a very sketchy view of the menu for the evening, I left her alone. At noon when I came down she told me she wasn't going to get dinner, perhaps that would bring L.E. to terms — with 10 coming for dinner — so I started in after lunch and cooked the whole thing from the roast duck on. When L.E. returned from town she called Mr. Whytock [the estate manager] over and he fired her immediately and Saturday a.m. Helen handed in her resignation. So I had to really *be cook — 12 for dinner on Sat. I ate with the guests on Sat. night at L.E. request . . . I made an orange pudding that she loved and also a beautiful sponge cake, and she told the guests that she couldn't go on a diet if Miss Brown was cooking.* (Dorothy Brown, May 1948, letter from Eaton Hall farm)

Relatives of Countess Vita Luettichau with Lady Eaton, front left, Eaton Hall, June 1948

Dorothy Brown did take time out from the backroom squabbles to enjoy some of the events from afar, however. She described the wedding of Austrian Prince Victor Hohenlohe to Countess Vita Luettichau that took place on June 6, 1948, in one of her letters home:

"For lunch we had hot consommé with cheese sticks, then all kinds of salads and garnishes — lobster, chicken, potato, dressed salmon and all kinds of garnishes, radishes, olives, devilled eggs, rye breads, etc. More champagne and Mother — I honestly didn't take a drop. For dessert, ice cream with frosted strawberry sauce, coffee and nuts and then a marvelous assortment of fancy cakes and cookies and wedding cake — it was wonderful . . ." (Dorothy Brown, June 6, 1948, letter from Eaton Hall farm)

Malt Bars, Buffeterias and Frozen Fricassee

While Lady Eaton maintained her position as head of the Eaton clan, entertaining employees and hosting elite social events, John David Eaton continued to expand the company's business across the country, adding dining rooms in Vancouver, London and Yorkdale and various other food services (catering, buffeterias, themed promotions) designed to meet the public's needs.

Vancouver was home to a number of Western-based department stores, so Eaton's profile had always been relatively low in the city. While there was a restaurant in the "old" Eaton's store, it was a basic room with bentwood chairs and white lighting fixtures reminiscent of a rather bleak school classroom. In the late 1940s Eaton's had built a major store in the city's downtown core. The restaurant in the new

Marine Room buffet, 1962

Portrait of Lady Eaton, 1940 Who's Who

location was characteristic of the store's high national standard: "Eaton's was a pioneer in providing excellent food at moderate prices in spacious, agreeable surroundings; first with the building of the stately Georgian Room in the Toronto Store in the early twenties; soon after in Winnipeg, Montreal and Hamilton stores; and in 1949, with the opening of the lovely, scenic Marine Room in the Vancouver Store" (*The Story of a Store: Eaton's of Canada, Serving the Nation*, 1959).

René Cera, the architect who had been instrumental in the original planning of the Georgian Room, also designed Vancouver's Marine Room. Cera's years with Eaton's afforded him knowledge and continuity, enabling him to bring the themes of elegance and fine service to his vision. The room's magnificent prospect over Vancouver Harbour allowed patrons to enjoy a superb view of the ocean, ships and mountains from the glassed-in restaurant, which occupied much of the top floor of the store. The room's proportions were intended to recreate those of a luxury liner's dining room.

The primrose colour scheme, chosen by Cera, gave the Marine Room a spacious, cheerful modern ambiance. The 500-seat room was carpeted throughout, providing an aura of quiet and comfort. Coastal

Marine Room poster, c. 1960

First Nations design influences were integrated into the décor. Different areas within the restaurant were named Discovery Bay, the Chart Room and the Flag Room, and made use of maps, charts and antique features to recreate local culture and history. The company was very proud of the restaurant's kitchens, among the largest in British Columbia. The bakery was staffed by a master baker with four assistants and four journeymen, who produced Eaton's chicken pies as well as all the desserts, Danish pastry, cakes, pies and puddings.

The Mayfair Room, London, Ontario, opening day, August 11, 1960

Eaton's new London store opened August 11, 1960. Dietitian Joan Caruso and manager Jim Matthews escorted Lady Eaton, now confined to a wheelchair, onto the new elevator. To their chagrin, the elevator stalled. When they finally arrived at the Mayfair Room, Lady Eaton admired the décor of the handsome new restaurant, also designed by René Cera. The room featured murals of five imaginary dancers — Lia, Matamoor, Daphne, Firebrand and Lydia — inspired by 17th-and 18th-century Italian *commedia dell'arte* design and by Ballets Russes designs from the 1920s. Gracing the entrance was a painting of the Firebird, from choreographer Michel Fokine's dance of the same name.

The Mayfair Room was in fact a "buffeteria," the first of Eaton's free-flow dining rooms, intended to replace the greater formality of rooms with table service. Equipped with the most modern equipment available, the kitchens had ovens with revolving trays, capable of baking bread for a whole community, and a six-speed cake mixer the size of a washing machine. The Wellington Square, London, Eaton's was the last new store Lady Eaton inspected.

Georgian Room cake counter sticker

Grabbing something on the run soon became a convenience Eaton's was happy to accommodate. Patrons often paused for a quick meal in the cafeterias and other food outlets. Toronto teenagers heading downtown could take the streetcar to the Annex loop, pick up a snack and head across the street to the movies. The malt bars and snack bars are remembered as a place for treats and breaks from the trials of shopping with adults. "From the shoe department we went straight to the Annex lunch counter. It was a stand-up counter with no stools. Aunt Hester treated herself and Mum to a red-hot and a Vernor's, and they both shared them with me" (Bernice Thurman Hunter, *That Scatterbrain Booky*, page 96).

Within the stores, the bakery counters offered a wide array of

World's largest china teapot, Commonwealth Week Eaton's tea promotion, 1961

products to take home, including cakes and pies, cookies and yeast products. The staff and printed materials informed customers which pies and cakes would last a day or two, and which should be eaten on the day purchased. Customers could order finger sandwiches, petits fours and tiny iced cakes for special occasions. Plates of these dainty "bridge sandwiches," six to a packet, were offered at the bakery counter.

Advances in refrigeration and freezing had made it possible to offer frozen food packages at the counters as of 1959. Customers could choose from a selection of early convenience food — Chicken in Fricassee Sauce, Beef and Vegetable Stew, Seafood Creole, Cheese Rarebit and Corned Beef Hash.

During the 1960s, customers bought exotic delicacies at the largest gourmet shop in Canada on the main floor of the Montreal store. In 1969, snails could be purchased there for $3.50 a dozen, while chocolate ants were priced at $2 a pound. Beer-fed massaged Kobe beef was available for $6.50 per pound. Despite these delicacies, things were a bit more straitlaced upstairs. True to Eaton's tradition, the ninth floor restaurant remained dry. Patrons quenched their thirst with tea and coffee and a variety of frosted summer drinks and sodas.

Georgian Room postcard, 1960s. "The Georgian Room, noted for its fine cuisine and gracious atmosphere. Styled on the lines of early Greece, with decor of pale green enhanced by sumptuous gold leaf."

A cross-country survey taken in 1968 calculated the volume of meals served in various Eaton's restaurants during 1967, Canada's Centennial Year. The numbers indicate Eaton's served up to 2 million customers annually, though Eaton's retail dominance in Canada was by then waning. The survey results, however, do attest to the continuing popularity of some of the dining rooms. In London, the Mayfair Room served 784,000 customers during Centennial Year. In Hamilton, the Green Room, luncheonette and staff cafeteria reported combined service of 549,400 meals. The Georgian Room served 228,900 meals, while the Round Room catered to 189,400 guests. In the Yorkdale store, the Vista Room, which had opened in 1964, catered to 681,000. In total, Eaton's restaurants served more than eight million customers in 1967.

The survey also logged information about a wide variety of other events and services in the dining rooms and cafeterias across the country: fashion shows, magic and puppet shows, Christmas and Easter shows, meetings of the Junior Quarterback Club, a children's television show, charm class graduations, a national sewing contest, business

Georgian Room Easter party, 1949

men's coffee clubs. Restaurant guests included Joey Smallwood, British Columbia premier and Mrs. W.A.C. Bennett, and hockey icon Gordie Howe.

The restaurants hosted many company promotional events. Eaton's attempted to cheat the long Canadian winter with its annual "Eaton's Uncrates the Sun" advertising campaign, which continued into the 1980s. Eaton's celebrated the cuisine of a different nation each year with special menus and banquets. Cookbooks with recipes from each year's featured nation helped to promote the events.

During the 1960s, John David Eaton's sons, John Craig, George, Frederik and Thor were employed in the family business and often ate lunch in the Georgian Room. When they did, the "boys" sat at a round table for eight to the right of the door. The staff always kept a tin of lobster, a favourite treat, on hand for them. Their father did not entirely approve, as lobster was expensive. They also ordered lunch to be delivered to them in their offices in the Annex building, some distance from the flagship store. While one of the boys was placing the order by telephone, another was heard shouting in the background, "Let's have lobster, Father's away!"

Eaton's Uncrates the Sun promotional pin

At an annual reception "for management and their wives" at Eaton Hall on September 12, 1960, Lady Eaton shared the reception line with John David and Signy Eaton. Guests were received quite formally. Hats and gloves were still the norm for women's dressy daywear, with fur stoles wrapped around the shoulders of many of the wives. The managers wore suits and ties. J.A. Brockie, who headed Public Relations, wrote an account:

A large marquee on the terrace was set up with long tea tables centred with arrangements of autumn-toned dahlias. Smilax twined around marquee poles and hanging baskets filled with yellow chrysanthemums and greenery added to the colourful setting as guests, numbering nearly 1,000, thronged the grounds. The green terraces of the estate and formal gardens made a

Eaton Hall reception "for managers and their wives," September 11, 1960

picturesque setting for the event with flower borders ablaze with colour. Chrysanthemums and flame-toned glads adorned the great hall, drawing room and ballroom. At the foot of the winding stairway a fountain was massed with gold-toned flowers and foliage."

The weather, reported Mr. Brockie's memo, was perfect. The reception menu was also on a grand scale, if rather standard party fare for the time. The Georgian Room supplied certain items for the menu, and the cost, to serve a thousand guests, was $3,214.

Menu for 1,000 Guests

Celery Hearts — Ripe and Stuffed Olives

Gherkins — Rose Radishes — Carrot Sticks

Sausage Rolls — Hot Cheese Puffs

Petit Chicken and Green Pepper Croquettes

Pineapple Wedges in Bacon

Broiled Stuffed Prunes — Tiny Lobster Patties

Wiener Tidbits — Devilled Eggs

Finger Rolls Stuffed with Foie Gras and Cress

Fresh Lobster Pieces (served on the shell)

Open Canapés

Smoked Salmon Curls

Asparagus Rolls

Smoked Turkey, Beef and Ham Sandwiches

Cheese and Ginger; Chicken Salad Sandwiches

Cucumber; Egg and Cress Sandwiches

Chilled Jumbo shrimps; Horseradish Sauce

Small Cocktail Biscuits

Cheese Trays

Variety of Fancy Small Cakes

Iced Petits Fours — Fruit Cake Fingers

Fruit and Marshmallow Balls

French Macaroons — Caramel and Lemon Tarts

Individual Ice Cream Fruits and Flowers

(Eaton's) Chocolate Ice Cream Squares

Salted Pecans — Peppermints

Tea — Coffee — Fruit Punch

Soft Drinks — Milk

Memory's Wall

Lady Eaton published her autobiography, *Memory's Wall*, at the age of 74 at her children's and grandchildren's gentle insistence, recasting memories recorded in a lifetime of journals to become a chronicle of a way of life quickly fading from view. *Memory's Wall* was Lady Eaton's first published work. *Rippling Rivers*, her memoir of her long New Brunswick fishing trip in 1917, was never in public circulation.

To promote the book, she toured nationally, travelling to the Maritimes in January and February of 1957, and in March and April of that year to Winnipeg, Saskatoon, Edmonton, Vancouver, Victoria and Calgary. She visited hospitals, attended private luncheons, addressed ladies' clubs, and was a guest on radio and television shows,

Portrait of Lady Eaton, 1960 Who's Who

as well as signing copies of her book in Eaton's stores across Canada. *Memory's Wall* quickly became a Canadian bestseller, going into its second printing within a week of publication.

Elizabeth Yorke, a vivid character and long-time manager with Eaton's Hostess Shop, was a friend of Lady Eaton's. This note, written by Miss Yorke for Lady Eaton's grandchildren, indicates the level of respect she garnered:

She was a beautiful woman, your grandmother, and had a most amazing sense of humour. She loved flowers and was a marvelous cook, because, like all normal healthy people she liked good food, and was among the first Canadians to see the possibilities in 'the home freezer' . . . She was a mischievous little child, and even then a traveller. She certainly slipped away from home and was always being pursued. Her sister Anna said, 'The reason I'm so thin is because in my youth I was constantly running after Flora.' She climbed trees, over the roofs of buildings, and was rarely without a huge bump on her head, and a pair of bruised and blackened knees. (Eaton's Archive)

Eaton's did maintain an "official biography" of Lady Eaton, which it used in its informational booklets and *The Story of a Store*. Lady Eaton's effects from Eaton Hall included notes in her writing composed for this purpose. They convey a sense of her own tastes and domestic practice, and her ongoing interest in food:

She has never ceased to try new recipes and methods, but is not fond of sweet foods. Therefore she does very little about them. She likes, as a pudding, good old-fashioned baked rice with a little sugar and no raisins, skim milk, rice, and slow cooking. The result is a creamy pudding with its own creamy sauce. Properly measured and cooked, then chilled, and with maple syrup it is food for the gods. She can also churn and make butter but she has never milked a cow . . . (Lady Eaton, Eaton Hall)

To the terror of restaurant staff, as well as keeping an eye on what was served on the menu, Lady Eaton always seemed to ask for something that was not on it. Once she requested a strawberry jam sandwich, which required the cook to spread Eaton's thick strawberry jam onto slices of thin white bread without tearing it.

Lady Eaton's cookbook collection was given to the public library in King City. The collection spans half a century, and reflects her lifelong interest in food and nutrition and her love of travel. One title, *Cook's Tour of European Kitchens: The Best Continental Dishes Suited to an English Table*, is a keepsake of her days in Italy, and is inscribed by the authors K. and M. von Shumacher as a *"souvenir des belles jours en Florence."* Another title, *Win's Whimsies*, is a collection of menus for various occasions, among them: Dinner for Eight, Sunday Luncheon, Dinner with a Curry, Dinner with Duck or Wild Game, Dinner à la Russe and Christmas Night When Everyone is Tired of Sweets. A tireless planner of social events, Lady Eaton was always on the lookout for innovative and interesting presentation ideas.

Her library also included two editions of *Quantity Cookery — Menu Planning and Cookery for Large Numbers*, by Lenore Richards and Nola Treat. These books, obviously much read, fall open at detailed charts and calculations, a reminder that domestic science was in its infancy in the early part of the 20th century. The book also provided material for Eaton's intern-training program. These American books were a strong influence in the early days of dietetics in Canada.

Lady Eaton also collected German, Jewish, American, Pennsylvania Dutch and Southern gourmet books, spiral-bound women's church and community group fundraising cookbooks, dieters' cookbooks and books of menus. They are reminders of days when moulded salads, mushrooms, tomatoes, asparagus and potatoes were the most common vegetables; when food was always prepared, rarely served whole and fresh; when Southern ladies had black cooks; when lunch, often called "dinner," was substantial, and men drove home for it; when chiffon pies came in every imaginable flavour — mocha and pineapple, pumpkin, strawberry and orange. Lady Eaton observed all these influences at her own table and in Eaton's restaurants.

Lady Eaton's love of travel and of occasion led to several trips across Canada and to Europe. Lady Eaton and many members of the family attended the coronation of Princess Elizabeth and the Duke of Edinburgh in London. Lady Eaton's rhapsodic description of the events was published in Eaton's employee newsletters. "All the world," she reported, "is uplifted by the vision of that young, beautiful, good woman" (*Flash*, 1951). Princess Elizabeth had toured Canada earlier that year, a cause for special menus and celebrations in Eaton's stores. The Winnipeg store produced a menu cover featuring a profile of the radiant young Princess and the Duke of Edinburgh, who visited the Winnipeg store on Tuesday, October 19, 1951.

Queen Elizabeth and Prince Philip's 1959 visit to Canada coincided with the opening of the St. Lawrence Seaway, a significant advance in Canada's shipping infrastructure. The dual celebration was marked with special exhibits and displays in Eaton's stores.

In 1961, the indomitable Lady Eaton undertook a tour of Madagascar, Egypt and Ethiopia. She wished to see the Nubian temples before they were swallowed forever by the construction of the Aswan

Dam. In 1962, at the age of 83, she made a tour of the Canadian Arctic, fulfilling a long-held desire to learn more about Inuit art and the people and land that shaped the sculptures she admired. The federal Department of Northern Affairs arranged accommodation for her, calling on the North West Mounted Police, the air force, and the army. Lady Eaton was wearing a leg brace while recovering from a broken right ankle, but set out with an ambitious itinerary. She and her companion visited Great Whale River on Hudson Bay, Fort Chimo, Frobisher Bay, Broughton Island, Hall Beach, Cambridge Bay, Baker Lake and Churchill, travelling 5,350 miles in 10 days, by airplane, jeep and freight canoe.

Lady Eaton carried fresh fruits and vegetables from Eaton Hall farm with her as gifts. While visiting Fort Chimo, she was entertained by the wife of the local Northern Affairs official, who matched Lady Eaton's gift of fresh produce, astonishingly, by offering a tossed green salad. Lady Eaton toured the local co-op and watched the processing of Arctic char and salmon caught in the Koksoak River. At Baker Lake, her pilot, "Captain Dill" Pickles, called ground control just three minutes before landing. The frantic operator relayed the news, and despite the scant warning, the ladies of Baker Lake rallied to provide Lady Eaton's party with a lunchtime feast of homemade bread, sandwiches, cookies and tea.

Lady Eaton was known as "Lady Eaton of Eaton's catalogue" by the people she met, who read the catalogue — and also used it to patch up their houses. *Time* magazine documented the trip with a photo in its September 1962 issue showing Lady Eaton in a tweed jacket and jodphurs and carrying one crutch. She stood beside an Inuit woman in beaded mukluks, a long skirt and a buttoned jacket, her head wrapped in a scarf.

Lady Eaton returned with a red parka, kamiks trimmed with white fur and a collection of Inuit sculpture from Frobisher Bay, Churchill, Fort Chimo, Hall Lake, Great Whale, Pangnurtung and Cape Dorset. The collection was first shown at the Royal Ontario Museum, then given as a gift to Trent University in 1964. More than 10 crates' worth of art were housed at Lady Eaton College, and known as the Lady Eaton Collection of Eskimo Art. Trent university is located in the Trent Valley, to the east of Omemee, the town where Lady Eaton was born and grew up. The university's mandate mirrors Lady Eaton's interests — the development of Canadian studies in history, culture and literature.

Although her beginnings were modest, Lady Eaton was not afraid to exercise her influence. More than once she appeared in the fur salon of a well-known Toronto store on the day of an important social event to acquire a wrap or coat, which would then be returned the following day.

Lady Eaton was very frank about her opinions, and often wrote letters to daily newspapers setting out her views on cultural and political matters. One version of her official biography stated that "in politics, she is a Conservative." It also suggested she was a rare combination of Saxon energy and Celtic versatility, a potent mix responsible for her public-spiritedness.

Lady Eaton's affection for the arts is also well documented. Eaton Auditorium was the venue for international guest artists, musicians, performers, actors and speakers. The hall was noted for its exceptional acoustic qualities and was Glenn Gould's favourite recording venue. In pre–Toronto Symphony Orchestra days, Lady Eaton was a friend of Reginald Stewart, pianist and first conductor of the Toronto Summer

Symphony. Stewart's first performances were given at Eaton Auditorium, but soon moved to Varsity Stadium to accommodate their popularity. Lady Eaton remained a strong symphony supporter.

She likewise helped to establish the National Theatre School and the Dominion Drama Festivals. She was founder and honorary president of the Canadian Players Foundation, started in 1960 and associated with the beginnings of the Stratford Festival. She delighted in attending Stratford opening nights, and was a regular patron until 1966, always sitting in the front row. The Festival presented her with a pair of white mute swans, which lived at the Eaton farm. She was also a patroness of New York City's Lincoln Center for the Performing Arts. Lady Eaton was a founding member of the Toronto Art Gallery and a life member of the Royal Ontario Museum.

Lady Eaton and Hunt Club friends. The Tally-Ho made an excellent vantage point for watching the hunt at Eaton Hall farm.

Lady Eaton was a keen rider, often seen on her Irish hunter, Paddy. She was honorary life master of the Fox Hounds of the Toronto and North York Hunt, the oldest such group in North America. Eaton Hall was frequently used as a destination for 15-mile chases through King Township. On his 80th birthday, Aemilius Jarvis, whose great-great-grandfather had convened the first Upper Canadian hunt in 1801, rode to hounds on his grey horse, and after a 10-mile chase, stood for two hours at a reception in his honour at Eaton Hall. Lady Eaton had arranged a large party, with tables set out in the shape of a horseshoe and a birthday cake featuring a rider on a grey horse and 80 candles.

Eaton Hall farm, 1925

As an honorary director of the Royal Winter Fair, Lady Eaton annually invited 240 or more guests to luncheons at Eaton Hall farm. She was a member of the Horse Show Association, and the Eaton Challenge Trophy was part of Royal Winter Fair tradition. Lady Eaton's horse, Rona, won the Governor General's Cup in 1958; a newspaper photograph from that time shows her accepting the cup from the Lieutenant-Governor, the Honorable Keiller McKay.

Lady Eaton was particularly proud of her fine herd of cows, established in 1921 at Eaton Hall farm, and in 1955 became the first woman to win the Master Breeder Award, the Holstein-Friesen Association's highest award. In 1966, she donated the herd of 78 dairy cows to a research project at the Ontario Agricultural College at the University of Guelph.

Lady Eaton was a member of numerous clubs and associations, including the Don Valley Conservation Association and the Men of the Trees. She was a patroness of the Ontario Rose Society and a life member of the Canadian Rose Society. At various times, she belonged to the York Club, the Granite Club, the Caledon Mountain and Trout, the Toronto Cricket, and Ontario Jockey Clubs, and the Eglinton Hunt. She was a member of the Women's Lyceum Club and the Ladies' Club, and a life member of the National Trust for Scotland and the Auxiliary Fund of the American School of Classical Studies in Athens, Greece.

True to her nursing background, Lady Eaton's interest in health care was ongoing. Sir John and Lady Eaton had made a gift of the surgical wing to Toronto General Hospital in 1913, in memory of Timothy Eaton. The Eaton Chair of Medicine at the University of Toronto, which attracted international attention as the first initiative of its kind, was established by the Eatons in 1922, a result of their shared interest in the study of child care. Lady Eaton became an honorary vice-president of the Red Cross, and was a patroness of Women's College Hospital. She was also closely identified with the Canadian National Institute for the Blind and with the Canadian National Committee for Mental Hygiene.

She was an honorary president of the United Welfare chest, and was associated with the Big Sister Association, the Casavant society and the Canadian Dietetic Association, attending most of the conferences. In 1949, she was named Dame of Grace of the Venerable Order of St. John of Jerusalem, at an investiture at Government House, Ottawa.

Lady Eaton was appointed a director of the national board of the Council of Christians and Jews on October 24, 1952, and received a human-relations citation. On that occasion, she reflected: "In my girlhood there was neither Greek, Roman, Jew nor Gentile, no V.O.N. or Red Cross. A team of men helped the doctor in disasters; women tended the sick. It was easy for me to accept the brotherhood of man."

In 1958, Lady Eaton bought St. Andrew's Everseley, a 110-year-old Presbyterian church not far from Eaton Hall, which was slated for demolition. Since then, the small stone chapel has been a popular setting for weddings. Lady Eaton was the first woman to be both a trustee and elder of Timothy Eaton United Church; in her honour, the community centre of the church, opened in 1962, is called the Flora McCrea Eaton Hall. The Eaton Family endowed a chapel in the church designed to focus attention on Holman Hunt's beautiful stained-glass window *The Light of the World.*

In recognition of her philanthropic contributions, Lady Eaton was awarded honorary doctorates by the University of Toronto, McGill University (following her endowment of the university's electronics lab), the University of Western Ontario, Waterloo Lutheran University and Bishop's University. Lady Eaton was also the recipient of Toronto's 1959 Civic Award of Merit.

In 1969, Eaton's celebrated 100 years of business. Lady Eaton was by then living in Toronto, so as a memento of the day of celebration, a copy of a ceremonial key used to open the Queen Street store was delivered to her at her home on Old Forest Hill Road. She often wore a brooch made of gold keys used at the openings of Eaton's in Winnipeg in 1905 and Eaton's College Street in 1930.

Lady Eaton died on July 9, 1970, at the age of 91. A thousand mourners attended the service for her at Timothy Eaton Memorial Church. Her place, the ninth pew on the west side of the sanctuary, was filled with pink roses. Following her death, memorial articles in newspapers across the country paid homage to her graciousness and her manifold achievements. Editorials cited her as "a woman of privilege" who made the best possible use of her stature in business to support her devotion to social causes and arts and culture in Canada. Lady Eaton counted the fine restaurants she envisioned and brought to life among her proudest achievements.

Portrait of Lady Eaton, 1969, Who's Who, *wearing the diamond maple leaves given to her by Sir John for her 1920 concert at Massey Hall*

Epilogue

In 1970, Eaton's Food Services office opened to standardize the company's national program. At this time, the restaurants also began to offer wine, beer and liquor, a true challenge to Eaton's tradition.

By this time, women shoppers had begun to opt for self-service, preferring to make selections from large displays of goods rather than count on personal attention in the stores or wait for mail-order delivery. Some of the stores began to downsize, alter their level of service or close completely.

From the mid-1970s into the 1980s, a trio of Sir John's restaurants, named for John Craig Eaton, operated briefly in Kitchener, at Winnipeg's Polo Park and in the men's fashions department of the Toronto Eaton Centre. Smaller than the spacious dining rooms of

Newly renovated CARLU, opened May 2003

Round Room, 1972

earlier eras, these were instead reminiscent of the Men's Grills. Diners were presented with oversized menu cards offering straightforward, robust menu selections. The concept was hearty and historic, with references to Eaton's past in the use of fonts on the menu, and in some of the dishes' names: Honey Glazed Ribs, Ground Beefsteak, Thick Ham Steak with Pineapple Ring and Raisin Sauce, and Chicken Pie.

Other Eaton's restaurants endured, were gradually redecorated or settled into a benign state of time warp. The Round Room was last redecorated in 1972, and closed in 1976.

During the 45 years that Eaton's occupied the store, the main-floor interiors illustrated here were gradually made tawdry by remodelling or neglect, especially during the '50s and early '60s, when the streamlined elegance of the '20s and '30s was at the nadir of its popularity. The seventh-floor interiors were also changed by the introduction of new colour schemes, the rebuilding of the Auditorium floor on a slope, and the removal of the fountain from the Round Room. When the store finally closed in 1976, the outlines of CARLU's design could still be seen, but it was difficult to sense the brilliance and high style of the original scheme. (William Dendy, *Lost Toronto,* page 162)

The Georgian Room and the Round Room offered a special menu for the last weeks they were open. The menu was nostalgic and simple, including chicken pie, salads and ice cream. The rooms closed

The Round Room

In 1930 when it opened, there couldn't have been a more up-to-the-minute place to go than Eaton's Round Room. Designed by Professor Jacques Carlu of Paris in the Art Deco style of the day – with exquisite murals by Mme. Carlu. It hasn't changed; we've come full circle. Deco is today's collectors' rage. And The Round Room is touted as one of the finest examples of the period in this country. Take a look before it closes (this Christmas Eve). In a sense, you're sitting down to dinner in the midst of art history.

The Georgian Room

On March 10, 1924 – with a flourish of fine linen, bone china and crystal – Eaton's opened The Georgian Room. There wasn't anything like her back in those days. And now, 52 years later – after countless Santa's breakfasts, Easter bunny lunches, fashion shows, teas and buffet suppers – she's about to close (on Christmas Eve '76). We'll miss her. But we're moving ahead (. . . and living up to our past). In February '77 you're invited – again – to come and try dining in a department store like you've never seen before. At Eaton's in the new Toronto Eaton Centre.

The Best Of Our Past.

Cream of Chicken Soup .70
Vegetable Soup .70
Chilled Juices .50
Fresh Grapefruit Sections .65
Iced Fruit Cocktail .80

INDIVIDUAL CHICKEN PIE, 3.35
Salad Greens

INDIVIDUAL STEAK & KIDNEY PIE, 3.35
Salad Greens

OMELETTE 3.50
Choice of Bacon and Chive, Mushroom, Cheddar Cheese or Spanish. Choice of Vegetable and Potato

ROAST SIRLOIN TIP OF BEEF 4.25
with Yorkshire Pudding, Choice of Vegetables and Potato

CHICKEN AND CELERY SALAD 3.60
delicately seasoned Chicken Salad served on Crisp Lettuce with Fruit and Vegetable Garnish

FRUIT SALAD PLATE 3.60
Selected Fruit, Cottage Cheese and Cream Dressing

SLICED CHICKEN SANDWICH PLATE 2.50
all white meat

HAM AND LETTUCE SANDWICH PLATE 2.50
with Mustard Pickles

Fresh Apple Pie .65
English Trifle .75
Ice Cream with Buffet Sundae Tray .85
Canadian or Blue Cheese with Fresh Fruit .75

Georgian Room and Round Room closing menu, December 1976

on Christmas Eve 1976, to make way for the opening of the shiny new Eaton Centre. The Eaton Centre's Dundas Room opened in 1977, replacing the Georgian Room as the flagship store's main restaurant.

In Montreal, Eaton's downtown restaurant enjoyed a different fate. The ninth floor was maintained, remaining relatively unchanged through the beginning of the 1980s, when its beautiful Art Moderne design once again became fashionable. Much of the original flatware and china was still in use. In 1980, Eaton's spent $30,000 to build an Art Deco buffet for the room. In 1981, the restaurant served about 700 lunches a day, with annual business of $1.3 million. Le 9e closed

The Vista Room, Yorkdale, 1964

in 1998. While the other floors of the landmark Eaton's building have been reconstructed as a honeycomb of fashion boutiques, plans to preserve the Montreal restaurant as a heritage site are being discussed.

The Vista Room at Yorkdale, renamed The Village Loft in 1968, operated a popular buffet service. Celebrations of Eaton's 125th anniversary were held there in 1994, and the restaurant lasted until the Yorkdale store's closure in 1998. London's Mayfair Room also closed in 1998.

On October 19, 1999, the Eaton's store in Winnipeg closed its doors. Despite the vigorous efforts of the city's outspoken "Save the Eaton's Building" coalition to preserve this heritage site, the focal point for retail and mail-order business in Western Canada for almost 100 years, the Winnipeg store was demolished during the winter of 2003.

Meanwhile, the Round Room, the seventh floor foyer and Eaton Auditorium at Toronto's College Park have been meticulously restored. The seventh floor reopened in May 2003 as The CARLU, a suite of elegant rooms extensively renovated by the firm ERA Architects. The space includes a foyer and concert hall, which accommodate private and corporate functions. The Round Room's Lalique fountain, once believed lost, and Natacha Carlu's murals have been restored to their original glamour. Perhaps the beautiful design and vibrant cultural life that enlivened these rooms will reinvigorate this site, recalling an era of immaculate presentation, detailed service and fastidious lunching.

Recipes

These recipes have been selected to represent favourite dishes served in the Eaton's restaurants. They exemplify those offered on Eaton's menus and include savoury recipes, salads, salad dressings, muffins, cookies, cakes, pies and ice cream sauces. The recipes come from dietitians' notes and private collections. They have been adapted for the home kitchen, in most cases scaled down from commercial quantities to quantities suitable for a family of four to six people. They have been very slightly updated where certain ingredients have either gone out of use or disappeared, such as a frozen egg-yolk and egg-white mixture, which was used in the production kitchens, or Holsum, a shortening substance. The recipes have been carefully tested by Katharine Mallinson, and thoughtfully tasted, in the time-honoured Eaton's tradition.

Original Georgian Room Chicken Pot Pie

1	pastry for one double-crust pie
4 cups	chicken stock
2 tbsp.	soft butter
2 tbsp.	chicken fat
8 tbsp.	all-purpose flour
1 cup	mushrooms — sliced
4 oz. jar	red pimento — drained and chopped
12	potato balls — steamed until just tender
1½	generous cups cooked white chicken meat in large pieces
1½	generous cups cooked dark chicken meat in large pieces

1. Prepare pastry for double-crust pie; set aside.

2. Fricassee Sauce: in a saucepan, blend butter, chicken fat and flour until smooth. Over medium heat, whisk in chicken stock. Simmer for 20 minutes until thickened. This sauce must be made fresh for pies the day they are to be eaten. Do not freeze.

3. In a 2-quart rectangular casserole dish, combine chicken and potatoes.

4. Stir mushrooms and pimento into Fricassee Sauce; pour over chicken and potatoes.

5. Roll pastry into a rectangle large enough to cover casserole dish, or cut into six 5-inch circles, and place on top of filling. Brush crust with egg and milk glaze (1 egg plus 1 tbsp. milk).

6. Bake at 450°F for 12 to 15 minutes or until pastry is golden brown and sauce bubbling.

Serves six. This can also be made as six individual 10 oz. pot pies.

Lady Eaton's Special-Order Crunchy Cheese Fingers

¼ cup	butter
½ lb.	cheddar cheese — grated
½ cup	fine corn-flake crumbs
¼ cup	cake or pastry flour
½ tsp.	salt
¼ tsp.	dry mustard powder
⅛ tsp.	paprika

1. Combine dry ingredients and set aside.

2. Cream the butter until quite soft, then mix in grated cheese. Add dry ingredients to make a crumbly dough.

3. Using fingers, press ingredients well together, working into a flat smooth shape.

4. On a floured surface, roll out as thin as possible. Cut into strips 2 inches long and ¾ inches wide.

5. Work up odd bits, roll and cut again until all mixture is used.

6. Place on a baking sheet lined with brown paper and bake at 400°F for 8 minutes. Serve warm or cold.

Toasted Cheese Dreams

½ lb.	Old Nippy cheddar cheese
3 oz.	imperial cheese
1 tsp.	dry mustard
1 tsp.	onion juice
1 tsp.	salt
drop	Tabasco sauce
½ tsp.	soy sauce
1	loaf fresh white bread, sliced lengthwise

1. Blend all ingredients in a food processor to make a spreadable mixture.

2. Cut crusts off bread. Run rolling pin over each slice.

3. Spread each slice of bread to edge with cheese filling. Tightly roll slices, being careful to keep sides in line. Wrap rolls individually in wax paper or plastic wrap, tightly securing ends. Refrigerate overnight.

4. Cut each roll into 8 slices. Place slices on cookie sheet and brush with melted butter. Broil until golden. Serve six toasted slices per person.

Makes 2-3 rolls.

Chicken Velvet Soup

3 tbsp.	butter
6 tbsp.	all-purpose flour
½ cup	warm milk
3 cups	hot chicken stock
½ cup	warm whipping cream
¾ cup	chopped cooked chicken
¼ tsp.	salt
dash	pepper

1. Melt butter in saucepan over medium heat; gradually stir in flour and cook for 3 minutes.

2. Gradually add 1 cup chicken stock, milk and cream. Cook, stirring constantly, until soup base is thick and smooth.

3. Whisk in remaining chicken stock and blend until smooth. Add chicken. Continue cooking until thoroughly heated. Season with salt and pepper and serve.

Iced Beet Borscht

4 cups	beef stock
1 cup	tomato juice
1½ tsp.	salt
1 cup	beet (finely shredded)
¼ cup	carrot (finely shredded)
½ cup	cabbage (finely shredded)
3 tbsp.	all-purpose flour
1½ tbsp.	soft butter
1 tsp.	sugar
1 tsp.	vinegar
1 tbsp.	whipped cream/bowl

1. Bring stock to boil. Add vegetables and simmer for 30 minutes or until vegetables are tender.

2. Heat tomato juice and stir in.

3. Mix flour and butter into a roux. Whisk into above mixture. Add sugar and vinegar.

4. Simmer 5 to 10 minutes.

5. Push through a fine sieve and chill.

6. Re-season if necessary. Serve cold with a tablespoon of whipped cream with each serving.

Georgian Room Chicken Salad

1 cup	diced cooked chicken
1 cup	diced celery
½ tsp.	chopped pimento
1½ tbsp.	Boiled Dressing (see page 166)
3 tbsp.	mayonnaise
½ tsp.	salt

1. Combine diced chicken, celery and pimento. Mix well.

2. Add dressing and mayonnaise. Add salt to taste.

3. Serve chilled.

Waldorf Salad

2 cups	diced apples (Northern Spy)
1 cup	diced celery
⅓ cup	walnut pieces
½ cup	Boiled Dressing (see page 166)
½ cup	unsweetened whipped cream

1. In a bowl, toss apples with celery and walnuts.

2. Dressing: in a chilled mixing bowl, whip cream to soft peaks. Fold in boiled dressing.

3. Fold dressing into apple mixture. Cover and chill until ready to serve.

Boiled Dressing – The Georgian Room c. 1952

¼ cup	all-purpose flour
1 tbsp.	dry mustard
1 tsp.	salt
½ rounded cup granulated sugar	
3	egg yolks (or 2 whole eggs)
1½ cups	milk
¾ cup	cider vinegar
¼ cup + 2 tbsp. butter	
pinch	cayenne (or white) pepper

1. Mix all dry ingredients in a heavy saucepan.

2. Beat eggs and milk together, then add to dry mixture in saucepan and combine. Stir in vinegar.

3. Bring mixture to boil over medium heat, stirring constantly. Simmer gently for 20 minutes, stirring occasionally. Remove from heat and stir in butter.

4. Chill and keep in refrigerator.

French Dressing

2 tbsp.	brown sugar
½ tsp.	salt
½ tbsp.	onion juice
¼ rounded tsp.	paprika
¾ cup	vegetable oil
¼ cup	malt vinegar

1. Combine brown sugar, salt, onion juice and paprika. Mix in vinegar.

2. Slowly beat in vegetable oil a few drops at a time.

Original Georgian Room Potato Salad

¼ cup	French Dressing (see page 167)
3 quarts	cooked and diced potatoes
3 tbsp.	chopped parsley
1 tbsp.	chopped green onion
¾ cup	Boiled Dressing (see page 166)
¾ cup	mayonnaise
2 cups	diced celery
	salt

1. Marinate warm diced potatoes in French Dressing.

2. While potatoes are marinating, chop parsley and onion, and dice celery.

3. Gently mix marinated potatoes with parsley, onion and celery, then fold in Boiled Dressing and mayonnaise. Add salt to taste.

4. Chill and keep in refrigerator until ready to serve.

Lady Eaton's Hot Potato Salad

9	medium-sized potatoes
4	eggs — hard boiled and chopped fine
½ (375 ml) jar	pimento olives — sliced thin
½ cup	sweet gherkin pickles — sliced thin
1 tbsp.	mayonnaise
1 cup	grated Old Nippy cheddar cheese
¼ cup	vinegar (from sweet gherkins)
6–8 strips	side bacon

1. Place potatoes in a medium saucepan with water to cover. Bring to boil; reduce heat and simmer for 20 to 25 minutes or until just tender. Drain and cool slightly. Peel and cube (½ –inch cubes).

2. Grease an oven casserole. Layer one-third of potatoes on bottom. Alternately layer one-half of eggs, olives, pickles and one-third of the cheese. Repeat layers, ending with a final layer of potatoes and remaining cheese.

3. Dressing: mix mayonnaise, pickle vinegar and liquid from the olive jar. Pour over salad and fold just to moisten.

4. Cover with bacon. Bake at 350°F for 30 minutes and until bacon is crisp. Serves 8.

Bran Muffins

3 cups	cake or pastry flour
3 cups	whole bran
1 cup + 2 tbsp.	wheat germ
¼ tsp.	baking soda
scant tsp.	salt
3 tbsp.	baking powder.
1 cup less 1 tbsp.	granulated sugar
1 cup + 2 tbsp.	skim-milk powder
3	eggs
1 ¼ cups	shortening, melted
1 tbsp.	molasses
2 cups	water

1. In a medium mixing bowl combine all dry ingredients. Make a well in centre of dry mixture.

2. In another mixing bowl combine egg, water and molasses.

3. Add liquid mixture and melted shortening all at once to dry mixture. Stir until just moistened (batter should be lumpy). Spoon batter into greased muffin tray, filling each two-thirds full.

4. Bake in a 375°F oven for 15 minutes.

Makes 2 dozen muffins.

Cheese Muffins

¾ cup shortening

¼ cup + 2 tbsp. sugar

2 eggs

4 tsp. baking powder

3 cups cake or pastry flour

½ tsp. salt

¾ cup skim milk

1½ cups cheddar cheese — grated

1. Cream shortening and sugar. Add eggs and continue creaming.

2. Add combined dry ingredients and skim milk alternately, starting and ending with dry ingredients. Add grated cheese to last dry addition, mixing just until blended.

3. Spoon batter into greased muffin cups, filling each two-thirds full.

4. Bake at 350°F for 15 to 20 minutes.

Makes 1 dozen muffins.

Cornmeal Muffins

1 cup	granulated sugar
½ cup	skim milk powder
½ tsp.	salt
2¼ cups	all-purpose flour
¾ cup	cornmeal
1 tbsp. + 2 tsp.	baking powder
¾ cup + 1 tbsp.	water
scant ½ cup	corn oil
2	eggs

1. Combine all dry ingredients in a medium-sized mixing bowl.

2. In a small mixing bowl combine beaten eggs, water and corn oil. Add all at once to dry ingredients.

3. Stir quickly until ingredients are just mixed and batter is lumpy in appearance.

4. Fill greased muffin pans two-thirds full and bake at 375°F for 15 to 20 minutes. Serve warm.

Makes 1 dozen muffins.

Canadian Honey Drops

3½ cups	all-purpose flour — sifted
2 tsp.	baking soda
1 cup	butter
1 cup	brown sugar
2	eggs
⅓ cup	honey
1 tsp.	vanilla extract
1 8-oz. jar	apricot jam

1. Sift together flour and baking soda. In a large bowl, beat together butter and brown sugar until light and fluffy. Add eggs, mixing well.

2. Stir in honey and vanilla.

3. Stir in sifted dry ingredients.

4. Chill dough until very firm. Pinch off a rounded teaspoon of dough and roll by hand into balls.

5. Bake at 350°F on an ungreased cookie sheet for 10 to 12 minutes.

6. Seal two cooled cookies together with apricot jam, and dust lightly with powdered sugar.

Makes 3 dozen filled cookies.

Gingersnap Cookies

2¼ cups	cake or pastry flour
2 tsp.	baking soda
1 tsp.	cinnamon
1 tsp.	cloves
1 tsp.	ginger
¾ cup	butter
1¼ cups	granulated sugar
4 tbsp.	molasses
1	egg

1. Sift flour, baking soda, cinnamon, cloves and ginger onto wax paper.

2. Beat butter with sugar in a large bowl until light and fluffy; beat in molasses and egg. Stir in flour mixture one-third at a time, blending well.

3. Chill overnight until firm enough to roll.

4. Roll out dough one-third at time on a well-floured board, to ⅛-inch thickness, cutting into fancy shapes with floured cookie cutters. Place cookies 1 inch apart on cookie sheet lined with parchment paper. Re-roll and cut out all trimmings.

5. Bake at 350°F for 7 to 9 minutes or until firm; cool cookies on wire racks.

Makes about 3½ dozen rolled and cut shapes.

Lady Eaton's Special-Order Oatmeal Cookies

2½ cups	pastry flour
½ tsp.	baking soda
1 (slightly rounded) tsp. baking powder	
1 tsp.	salt
1¼ cups	shortening
2 tbsp.	butter
2⅓ cups	brown sugar — firmly packed
1	egg
1 cup	milk
3⅓ cups	quick-cooking rolled oats

1. Measure all dry ingredients except oats into a sifter.

2. Beat shortening and butter with brown sugar in a large bowl until light and fluffy; beat in egg and milk. Sift in flour mixture, blending well. Fold in oats.

3. Drop by tablespoon onto cookie sheet lined with parchment paper.

4. Bake at 375°F for 10 to 12 minutes, let stand 1 minute on cookie sheet. Cool completely on wire rack.

Makes about 6 dozen cookies.

Marshmallow Sauce

1½ tsp.	gelatin
2 tbsp.	cold water
1⅓ cup	granulated sugar
1 cup	corn syrup
¼ cup	hot water
½ tsp.	vanilla extract

1. Soak gelatin in cold water.
2. Boil sugar, syrup and hot water to 220°F on a candy thermometer.
3. Pour hot syrup over gelatin.
4. Beat with an electric mixer for 10 minutes.

In the College Street store, the small bowls used for sauce in the Round Room were recycled from an earlier era; they were the original Georgian Room finger bowls.

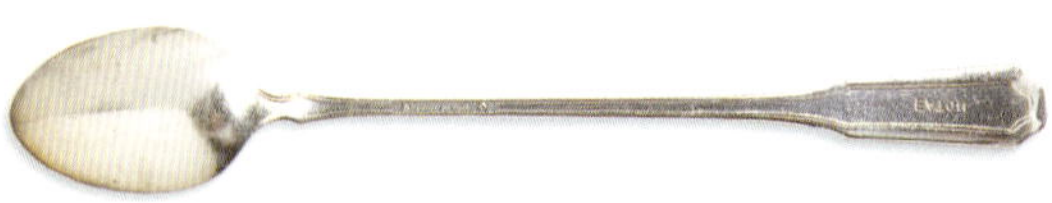

Chocolate Sauce

1¾ cup + 1 tbsp. granulated sugar

½ cup water

2 oz. unsweetened chocolate — melted

1½ cups corn syrup

½ tsp. vanilla extract

¼ tsp. salt

1. Boil sugar and water to 220°F on a candy thermometer.

2. Add to melted chocolate very slowly. Add corn syrup.

3. Cool. Add vanilla and salt. Mix thoroughly.

Butterscotch Sauce

1 cup	firmly packed brown sugar
½ cup + 2 tbsp.	corn syrup
⅛ tsp.	salt
¼ cup	soft butter
½ cup	whipping cream
½ tsp.	vanilla extract

1. In a small saucepan mix sugar, syrup and salt.

2. Boil until mixture reaches 248°F on a candy thermometer.

3. Remove from heat, add butter and allow to cool.

4. Add cream very slowly, stirring in by hand.

5. Add vanilla. Mix thoroughly.

Montreal Gingerbread

2½ cups	all-purpose flour
1½ tsp.	baking soda
¼ tsp.	salt
2 tsp.	ginger
½ tsp.	cinnamon
½ tsp.	cloves
½ tsp.	nutmeg
½ tsp.	baking powder
2	eggs
¾ cup	molasses
¾ cup	dark brown sugar
¾ cup	butter — melted
¾ cup	boiling water

1. Sift dry ingredients together and set aside.

2. In a large bowl, beat eggs well. Add molasses, sugar and melted butter.

3. Stir in sifted dry ingredients by hand.

4. Add and gradually mix boiling water in by hand.

5. Bake in a greased 9 x 13-inch pan for 30 to 40 minutes or until centre springs back when lightly pressed with fingertip.

6. Cool cake in the pan on wire rack for 10 minutes; loosen around edges with a knife; turn out onto wire rack to cool. Serve warm or cool, with whipped cream.

Georgian Room Chocolate Cake

3 squares	unsweetened chocolate — melted
2¼ cups	cake or pastry flour
1¼ tsp.	baking soda
¼ tsp.	salt
½ cup	butter
1¼ cups	firmly packed light brown sugar
2	eggs
1 cup + 3 tbsp.	buttermilk
1 tsp.	vanilla extract

1. Melt chocolate in a double-boiler over, but not in, boiling water.

2. Sift flour, baking soda and salt onto wax paper.

3. In a large bowl, cream butter, add sugar gradually and beat until light and fluffy; add eggs and continue creaming. Add chocolate.

4. Add flour mixture alternately with buttermilk and vanilla, starting and ending with flour.

5. Pour into two greased or floured pans, spreading mixture evenly.

6. Bake at 350°F for 30 to 35 minutes or until centre springs back when lightly pressed with fingertip.

7. Cool on wire racks; when cool remove cakes from pans. Cool completely on wire racks.

8. Frost with chocolate cream icing.

Makes one 8-inch double-layer cake.

Chocolate Cream Icing

2 cups icing sugar

2 egg yolks

4 tbsp. butter — soft, but not melted

1 tsp. vanilla extract

4 squares unsweetened melted chocolate

½ cup milk

Put all ingredients in mixing bowl and beat until consistency of whipped cream.

Coffee Velvet Pie

1 tbsp.	gelatin
¼ cup	cold water
4	egg yolks
½ cup	granulated sugar
pinch	salt
1½ cups	milk
1 tsp.	vanilla extract
4	egg whites
4 tsp.	instant coffee
to taste	nutmeg
½ cup	semisweet chocolate pieces
1	pre-baked pastry shell

1. Soften gelatin in the cold water.

2. In top of double-boiler beat egg yolks with sugar and salt. In a small saucepan, scald milk and mix slowly into egg yolk mixture. Add gelatin to warm mixture and cook over, but not in, boiling water until mixture thickens and coats back of wooden spoon. Stir in vanilla. Remove from heat. Allow to cool and set until mixture mounds when dropped from spoon.

3. Beat egg whites with coffee until foamy. Slowly beat in remaining ¼ cup of sugar until meringue stands in stiff peaks. Fold meringue into cooled custard until no streaks remain. Pour into prepared pastry shell.

4. Dust top of pie with nutmeg and allow to set partially.

5. Melt chocolate and mix in 8 tsp. of water, or until thin enough to drizzle over pie.

6. Chill pie until completely set (about 6 hours).

Butterscotch Pie

Filling

1 cup	dark brown sugar — firmly packed
6 tbsp.	all-purpose flour
¼ tsp.	salt
2 cups	whole milk
6 tbsp.	butter
3	egg yolks
1 tsp.	vanilla extract
1	pre-baked pie shell

1. In a mixing bowl, make a smooth paste of flour, and 3 tbsps. of brown sugar. Add salt and ⅔ cup of milk.

2. In a heavy saucepan melt butter and balance of brown sugar. Cook, stirring over medium heat, until smooth and well blended, to develop butterscotch flavour (about 10 minutes). Add the rest of the milk and cook over medium heat until butterscotch is dissolved.

3. Stir a small amount of the hot mixture into flour and milk paste, and then add to butterscotch mixture in saucepan. Cook over medium heat until thick and flour taste is gone, stirring constantly (15 to 20 minutes).

4. Beat egg yolks in separate bowl and gradually stir in small amounts of hot butterscotch mixture. Add egg mixture to remaining cooked mixture in saucepan and cook until temperature reaches 165°F on a candy thermometer, stirring all the while.

5. Remove from heat and add vanilla. Pour into cooled pie shell and top with meringue.

Meringue

3	egg whites (at room temperature)
6 tbsp.	sugar

1. Beat egg whites at high speed until frothy and starting to peak.

2. At medium speed, add sugar 1 tbsp. at a time, and beat at high speed until stiff and glossy.

3. Pile meringue onto filling, spreading to edge of crust.

4. Bake at 350°F for 12 to 15 minutes or until golden.

Raspberry Bavarian Pie

1 tbsp.	gelatin
3 tbsp.	cold water
1 cup	granulated sugar
pinch	salt
⅔ cup	water
1 pint	frozen raspberries
½ tsp.	lemon juice
1 cup	whipping cream
¼ tsp.	vanilla extract
1	pre-baked pie shell

1. In a small bowl, sprinkle gelatin over 3 tbsp. of cold water.

2. In a small saucepan, dissolve sugar, salt and balance of water and bring just to boiling point. Remove from heat, and dissolve gelatin in hot sugar syrup.

3. Add almost-defrosted berries and lemon juice to sugar syrup and allow this mixture to set and cool to a soft jelly stage.

4. Beat with electric mixer at medium speed until smooth.

5. In a separate bowl, whip cream until stiff and fold into raspberry mixture. Pour into cooled baked pie shell and refrigerate for 6 hours, or until set.

Christmas Cake — Dark Fruit Cake

1 lb.	butter
1 lb.	granulated sugar
8	eggs
2 lbs.	raisins
2 lbs.	currants
1 lb.	mixed candied peel, chopped
½ lb.	almonds
1½ lbs.	dates, chopped
½ lb.	glazed red and green cherries
¾ tbsp.	cinnamon
¾ tbsp.	nutmeg
¾ tbsp.	cloves
1 lb.	all-purpose flour
½ tsp.	baking soda
½	lemon, both juice and rind
½ cup	grape or pineapple juice

1. Prepare fruit by washing raisins and currants. Cut cherries in half; blanch almonds and split in half.

2. Dry washed fruit thoroughly and mix fruit, nuts and peel with part of the flour, so that each piece is separate and coated with flour.

3. Cream butter; add sugar gradually, beating well after each addition. Beat eggs and add.

4. Sift remaining flour with spices and soda into butter mixture, adding alternately with fruit juice.

5. Stir in fruit and mix until completely blended.

6. Pour into prepared cake pans lined with 3 layers of brown paper with a top layer of greased wax paper.

7. Bake at 250°F for approximately 3 hours, or until cake is firm and no longer sizzles when pressed lightly with fingertip. Cool on cake rack until thoroughly cooled. Wrap in foil and store in a cake tin.

Makes 2 large cakes, or 1 large cake and 12 small gift-sized loaves.

To this recipe may be added any or all of the following:

⅛ lb. glazed pineapple
⅛ lb. candied ginger
½ cup grape jelly
1 oz. melted chocolate

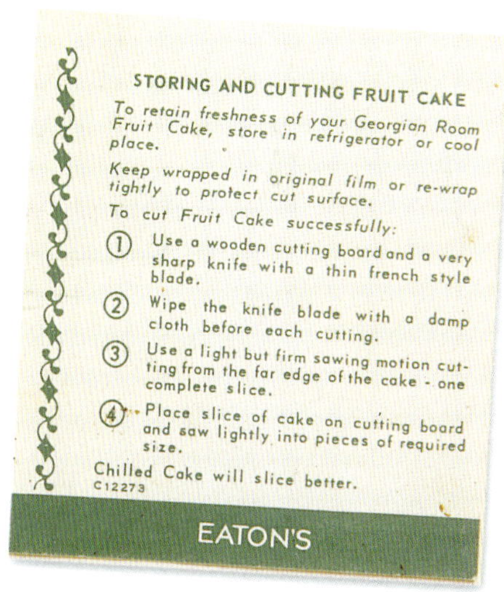
STORING AND CUTTING FRUIT CAKE

To retain freshness of your Georgian Room Fruit Cake, store in refrigerator or cool place.

Keep wrapped in original film or re-wrap tightly to protect cut surface.

To cut Fruit Cake successfully:

1. Use a wooden cutting board and a very sharp knife with a thin french style blade.
2. Wipe the knife blade with a damp cloth before each cutting.
3. Use a light but firm sawing motion cutting from the far edge of the cake - one complete slice.
4. Place slice of cake on cutting board and saw lightly into pieces of required size.

Chilled Cake will slice better.

C12273

EATON'S

Shortbread

1 cup butter

½ cup fruit sugar

or

⅔ cup brown sugar

2¼ cups all-purpose flour

1. Preheat oven to 300°F.

2. Cream butter until very light and then slowly blend in sugar. Beat until light and fluffy.

3. Stir flour in gradually. Knead well to blend in the last of the flour. Chill for 30 minutes.

4. Roll dough out on lightly-floured surface ¼-inch thick and cut into fancy shapes or squares. Pick with a fork.

5. Bake on ungreased baking sheet in 300°F oven for 18 to 20 minutes, or until set but not browned.

Makes 5 dozen.

Queen Elizabeth Cake

Coconut-Date Cake

1 cup	dates
1 cup	boiling water
½ tsp.	baking soda
¼ cup	butter
1 cup	granulated sugar
1 tsp.	vanilla extract
1⅓ cups	white flour
½ tsp.	salt
½ tsp.	baking powder

Topping

¾ cup	unsweetened flaked coconut
4 tbsp.	butter
6 tbsp.	brown sugar
2 tbsp.	milk or cream

1. Boil dates and water to make a paste. Add baking soda to hot mixture.

2. Cream butter, sugar and vanilla. Combine with date mixture.

3. Sift together flour, salt and baking powder. Add to mixture.

4. Bake at 350°F for 30 to 40 minutes, until cake springs back lightly to the touch.

5. Prepare topping. Boil all topping ingredients together for 3 minutes, stirring constantly. Spread on cake while still warm. Return cake to oven and broil until brown and sizzling (about 5 minutes).

Christmas Pudding, 1929–1934

(Makes 25 1-lb puddings)

		UNIT COST	TOTAL COST
Monarch pastry flour	2 lbs.	.026 lb.	.052
bread crumbs	2 lbs.	.08 lb.	.160
brown sugar	2 lbs.	.047 lb.	.094
fruit sugar	2 lbs.	.06 lb.	.120
salt	5 tbsp.	.02 lb.	.005
suet	3 lbs.	.08 lb.	.210
lemon peel	10 oz.	.14 lb.	.088
orange peel	10 oz.	.17 lb.	.110
candied peel	12 oz.	.22 lb.	.170
blanched almonds	1 lb.	.28 lb.	.280
sultana raisins	4 lbs.	.11 lb.	.440
seeded raisins	4 lbs.	.11 lb.	.440
currants	4 lbs.	.115 lb.	.460
nutmeg	1 tbsp.	.25 lb.	.009
mixed spice	5 tsp.	.115 lb.	.008
lemon rind	4 oz.	.05 oz.	.200
eggs	16	.18 doz.	.240
lemon juice	4 tbsp."	.11 cup	.028
cider	3 cups	.35 gallon	.066
Cost of 25 1-lb puddings			3.180
Cost of 1 1-lb pudding		.127	

Method

1. Mix sifted dry ingredients.
2. Add sugar, crumbs and rind.
3. Add dredged fruit and nuts.
4. Add suet and mix thoroughly.
5. Add beaten eggs, lemon juice and cider.
6. Scale off into cotton sheeting and tie tightly.
7. Boil for 3 to 5 hours, depending on size.
8. Hang to dry, being careful that they do not touch each other to produce mould.

Hard Sauce for 100 servings

1 lb	butter
3 lbs.	fruit sugar
1 tbsp.	lemon juice
1 tbsp.	vanilla extract
2 tsp.	salt

Lemon Butter Sauce (1 gallon)

3 oz.	Monarch pastry flour
3 lbs.	sugar
2 cups	cold water
5 pts.	hot water
1 oz.	lemon rind
1 tbsp.	salt
1 lb.	butter
1 cup	lemon juice

Nutmeg Sauce (1½ gallons)

9 oz.	flour
6 lbs.	granulated sugar
4 cups	cold water
6 pts.	hot water
1 lb.	butter
2 tbsp.	salt
2 tbsp.	vanilla extract
2 tbsp.	nutmeg

Round Room Red Velvet Cake

½ cup	shortening
1½ cups	granulated sugar
2	eggs
2 tbsp.	unsweetened cocoa
2 tbsp.	red food colouring
½ tsp.	salt
1 tsp.	vanilla extract
2½ cups	all-purpose flour — sifted
1 cup	buttermilk
1½ tsp.	baking soda
1 tbsp.	vinegar

Frosting

5 tbsp.	all-purpose flour
1 cup	milk
1 cup	butter — softened
1 cup	granulated sugar
1 tsp.	vanilla extract

1. In large bowl, cream together shortening and sugar until light and fluffy. Add eggs, beating well. Make paste with cocoa and food colouring. Add to egg mixture. Add salt and vanilla. Alternately add flour and buttermilk, beginning and ending with flour.

2. Mix baking soda and vinegar. Fold into mixture; do not beat.

3. Pour batter into two greased 9-inch pans. Bake in 350°F oven for 30 to 35 minutes, or until tester inserted in centre comes out clean. Cool on wire racks. When cool, remove cakes from pan and split each into two layers.

4. Frosting: in small saucepan, combine flour and milk. Cook until very thick. Cool.

5. In medium bowl, cream butter, sugar and vanilla until fluffy. Add flour/milk paste a spoonful at a time, beating until the consistency of whipped cream (mixture looks curdled at first).

6. Spread between layers, and on top and sides of cake.

Makes 12 servings.

This cake was an *exclusive* sweet recipe of Eaton's, and employees who knew the recipe were bonded in silence. Bakery workers who prepared the Red Velvet Cake could neither sell nor reveal the recipe, which was kept locked away. The origins of this recipe also remain a little mysterious. The Red Velvet Cake is said to have originated in the 1940s at the Waldorf Astoria Hotel in New York City, but others attribute it to the Southern United States. In Southern recipes, beets are one of the ingredients that give the cake its distinctive colour. The four-layer Red Velvet Cake was very expensive to produce. It was offered in a number of different sizes at the cake counters. Along with Maryanns, or Empire cookies — an iced, jam-filled cookie — and petits fours, the Red Velvet Cake was a much-loved treat.

Sources

Buik, Helen, "Making Food Worth Talking About." *Journal of the American Dietetic Association.* Vol. 33, No. 2, February 1957.

Carlu, Jacques, "The Montreal Store of T. Eaton & Co." *The Architectural Record.* Vol. 69, No. 6, June 1931.

Dendy, William, *Lost Toronto.* Toronto: Oxford University Press, 1978.

"The Eaton's You'll Never See." *Globe and Mail,* August 4, 1945.

Eaton, Flora McCrea, *Memory's Wall: The Autobiography of Flora McCrea Eaton.* Toronto: Clarke Irwin & Company, 1956.

Francis, Jean, *A Treasury of Eaton's Beauty Dolls.* Wellington, ON: published by the author, 1998.

Hunter, Bernice Thurman, *That Scatterbrain Booky.* Toronto: Scholastic Canada, 1981.

Lang and Upton, eds., *The Dietetic Profession in Canada.* Toronto: Canadian Dietetic Association, 1973.

Macpherson, Mary-Etta, *Shopkeepers to a Nation: The Eatons.* Toronto: McClelland & Stewart, 1963.

McQueen, Rod, *The Eatons: The Rise and Fall of Canada's Royal Family.* Toronto: Stoddart Publishing Co., 1998.

Santink, Joy L., *Timothy Eaton and the Rise of His Department Store.* Toronto: University of Toronto Press, 1990.

Stephenson, William, *The Store that Timothy Built.* Toronto: McClelland & Stewart, 1969.

Eaton's Publications

Bricks, Dreams & People: The Magic Circle 1971-72. Toronto: Eaton's, 1972.

Facts About Eaton's. Winnipeg: Eaton's, 1923.

Flash. Toronto: Eaton's, September 1937, November 1950, January 1951, November 1954, November 1955.

General Instructions and Rules for the Guidance of Waitresses. Toronto: Eaton's, 1965.

Notes on How to Obtain Quality in Food. Toronto: Eaton's, 1934 (2109-6/10/34-IM-EIO).

The Home Comers. Toronto: Eaton's, 1903.

The Scribe, *Golden Jubilee 1869-1919: A Book to Commemorate the Fiftieth Anniversary of the T. Eaton Co. Limited.* Toronto: Eaton's, 1919.

The Story of a Store. Toronto and Winnipeg: Eaton's, 1910, 1959, 1968.

With Our Compliments. Toronto: Eaton's, 1930.

Other Sources

Archives of the City of Vancouver

Archives of Trent University, Peterborough, Ontario

Collections, City of Toronto Culture Division

Dance Collection Danse Archives

Eaton's Archives at the Archives of Ontario

http://calgarypubliclibrary.com/eaton

http://indexes.tpl.toronto.on.ca/archindont (The Architectural Index for Ontario, Jacques Carlu)

http://lg.gov.mb.ca/speech/2000/novdec/

http://www.mts.net/~heritag2

Martin, Catherine. *The Ladies of the 9th Floor.* Montreal: CBC, 1998.

Photo Credits

Chapter I

page 2 T. Eaton Co., fonds, F-229-308-0-2320-3, Archives of Ontario
page 5 T. Eaton Co., fonds, F-229-308-0-7, Archives of Ontario
page 6 T. Eaton Co., fonds, F-229-308-0-2329, Archives of Ontario
page 8 T. Eaton Co., fonds, F-229-162-0-1377, Archives of Ontario
page 9 T. Eaton Co., fonds, F-229-308-0-2320-1, Archives of Ontario
page 10 T. Eaton Co., fonds, F-229-308-0-2319-1, Archives of Ontario
page 11 T. Eaton Co., fonds, F-229-308-0-2304, Archives of Ontario
page 12 T. Eaton Co., fonds, F-229-308-0-2321-2, Archives of Ontario
page 13 T. Eaton Co., fonds, F-229-308-0-2321-1, Archives of Ontario
page 14 T. Eaton Co., fonds, F-229-308-0-11-2, Archives of Ontario

Chapter II

page 16 Miriam Adams
page 19 T. Eaton Co., fonds, F-229-308-0-1498-1, Archives of Ontario
page 21 T. Eaton Co., fonds, F-229-308-0-181-20, Archives of Ontario
page 23 T. Eaton Co., fonds, F-229-308-0-1999, Archives of Ontario

Chapter III

page 24	T. Eaton Co., fonds, F-229-308-0-2438, Archives of Ontario
page 29	T. Eaton Co., fonds, F-229-308-0-1263, Archives of Ontario
page 31	T. Eaton Co., fonds, F-229-308-0-1338-1, Archives of Ontario
page 32	T. Eaton Co., fonds, F-229-308-0-2254, Archives of Ontario

Chapter IV

page 38	T. Eaton Co., fonds, F-229-308-0-2307-3, Archives of Ontario
page 40	T. Eaton Co., fonds, F-229-221-0-99, Archives of Ontario
page 41	T. Eaton Co., fonds, F-229-308-0-1988, Archives of Ontario
page 42	T. Eaton Co., fonds, F-229-308-0-2322-1, Archives of Ontario
page 44	T. Eaton Co., fonds, F-229-162-0-1374, Archives of Ontario
page 45	T. Eaton Co., fonds, F-229-162-0-1374, Archives of Ontario
page 46	Donna Griffith
page 46	Donna Griffith
page 47	Donna Griffith
page 47	Donna Griffith
page 48	T. Eaton Co., fonds, F-229-308-0-2309-1, Archives of Ontario
page 49	T. Eaton Co., fonds, F-229-308-0-2309, Archives of Ontario
page 50	T. Eaton Co., fonds, F-229-308-0-2308-1, Archives of Ontario
page 51	T. Eaton Co., fonds, F-229-162-0-1373, Archives of Ontario
page 52	Donna Griffith

Chapter V

page 54	T. Eaton Co., fonds, F-229-308-0-1984, Archives of Ontario
page 57	T. Eaton Co., fonds, F-229-308-0-2300-1, Archives of Ontario
page 58	T. Eaton Co., fonds, F-229-308-0-1991, Archives of Ontario
page 59	T. Eaton Co., fonds, F-229-308-O-1999, Archives of Ontario
page 60	T. Eaton Co., fonds, F-229-162-0-1372, Archives of Ontario
page 61	Donna Griffith

Chapter VI

page 62	T. Eaton Co., fonds, F-229-308-0-2326-2, Archives of Ontario
page 64	T. Eaton Co., fonds, F-229-308-0-1522, Archives of Ontario
page 65	T. Eaton Co., fonds, F-229-308-0-515, Archives of Ontario
page 66	Toronto Reference Library
page 67	T. Eaton Co., fonds, F-229-308-0-2325-1, Archives of Ontario
page 69	T. Eaton Co., fonds, F-229-308-0-2326-4, Archives of Ontario
page 71	T. Eaton Co., fonds, F-229-162-0-1380, Archives of Ontario

page 72	T. Eaton Co., fonds, F-229-162-0-1358, Archives of Ontario
page 73	T. Eaton Co., fonds, F-229-308-0-2336-3, Archives of Ontario
page 74	T. Eaton Co., fonds, F-229-162-0-1358, Archives of Ontario

Chapter VII

page 76	T. Eaton Co., fonds, F-229-308-0-1292-1, Archives of Ontario
page 79	T. Eaton Co., fonds, F-229-304-1-8-1, Archives of Ontario

Chapter VIII

page 84	T. Eaton Co., fonds, F-229-305-1-17, Archives of Ontario
page 86	T. Eaton Co., fonds, F-229-193, Archives of Ontario
page 87	T. Eaton Co., fonds, F-229-308-0-733-2, Archives of Ontario
page 88	T. Eaton Co., fonds, F-229-308-0-736-1, Archives of Ontario
page 89	Donna Griffith
page 90	Donna Griffith
page 91	Donna Griffith
page 92	T. Eaton Co., fonds, F-229-162-0-1376, Archives of Ontario
page 93	T. Eaton Co., fonds, F-229-308-0-1376, Archives of Ontario
page 94	T. Eaton Co., fonds, F-229-162 -0-1373, Archives of Ontario
page 95	T. Eaton Co., fonds, F-229-162-0-532, Archives of Ontario

Chapter IX

page 96	T. Eaton Co., fonds, F-229-308-0-2311, Archives of Ontario
page 98	T. Eaton Co., fonds, F-229-308-0-2300-2, Archives of Ontario
page 99	T. Eaton Co., fonds, F-229-308-0-2310-1, Archives of Ontario
page 107	T. Eaton Co., fonds, F-229-308-0-1989-1, Archives of Ontario
page 108	T. Eaton Co., fonds, F-229-308-0-2311, Archives of Ontario
page 110	T. Eaton Co., fonds, F-229-308-0-2311, Archives of Ontario
page 111	T. Eaton Co., fonds, F-229-162-0-1373, Archives of Ontario
page 112	T. Eaton Co., fonds, F-229-308-0-2311, Archives of Ontario
page 120	Donna Griffith
page 122	Donna Griffith

Chapter X

page 124	T. Eaton Co., fonds, F-229-308-0-2296-1, Archives of Ontario
page 126	T. Eaton Co., fonds, F-229-221-0-99, Archives of Ontario
page 127	T. Eaton Co., fonds, F-229-308-0-2297, Archives of Ontario
page 128	T. Eaton Co., fonds, F-229-308-0-2302, Archives of Ontario
page 129	Donna Griffith

page 130	T. Eaton Co., fonds, F-229-304-1-12-1, Archives of Ontario
page 131	Donna Griffith
page 132	T. Eaton Co., fonds, F-229-308-0-2236, Archives of Ontario
page 133	Donna Griffith
page 134	T. Eaton Co., fonds, F-229-308-0-1325-1, Archives of Ontario

Chapter XI

page 136	T. Eaton Co., fonds, F-221-308-0-99, Archives of Ontario
page 143	T. Eaton Co., fonds, C7-3, 24079H, Archives of Ontario
page 144	T. Eaton Co., fonds, F-229-308-0-11-1, Archives of Ontario
page 147	T. Eaton Co., fonds, F-229-221-0-99, Archives of Ontario

Epilogue

page 148	Chris Ponce/Envision
page 150	T. Eaton Co., fonds, F-229-308-0-2328-1, Archives of Ontario
page 152	Donna Griffith
page 153	T. Eaton Co., fonds, F-229-308-0-2331-1, Archives of Ontario

Food Photography

All photography in this section by Donna Griffith. Food Styling by Katharine Mallinson. Georgian Room Fruit Salad made by Joan Caruso.

page 156	Round Room Red Velvet Cake
page 157	Georgian Room Fruit Salad
page 158	Original Georgian Room Chicken Pot Pie
page 163	Iced Beet Borscht and Chicken Velvet Soup
page 170	Bran Muffins, Cheese Muffins, Cornmeal Muffins
page 176	Canadian Honey Drops, Gingersnap Cookies, Lady Eaton's Special-Order Oatmeal Cookies
page 179	Ice Cream spoons
page 188	Coffee Velvet Pie, Raspberry Bavarian Pie
page 190	Christmas Cake — Dark Fruit Cake
page 191	Storing and Cutting Fruit Cake
page 196	Round Room Red Velvet Cake

Acknowledgements

Photographs from the T. Eaton Company Limited archive records in the Archives of Ontario are used with the generous permission of Sears Canada Inc. Quotes from *Lost Toronto* © William Dendy 1978 are used with the generous permission of Oxford University Press Canada. The quote from *That Scatterbrain Booky* is used by generous permission of Scholastic Canada Ltd. Items from private collections are used with the generous permission of Joan Caruso, Dorothy Ferguson, Marjorie Jackson and Jim Matthews.

Thank you to Evlyn Payton Tayler for memories of her granny Lady Eaton's love of impeccable presentation, and for memories of the Round Room, the Georgian Room and Le 9e; Joan Caruso, long-time dietitian in Eaton's restaurants, for recipe consultation, generous supplies of archival materials, leads, ongoing enthusiasm, valuable comments and access to Elsie Applegarth's collection; Marjorie Jackson and Dorothy Ferguson (née Brown), former Eaton's dietitians, for sharing letters and mementos, notes, books and memories; Verna Mathews and Jim Matthews, Eaton's memorabilia collector extraordinaire; Judith McErvel, former Eaton's archivist; Carmel Neighbourhood, for memories of Winnipeg's bakery; Betty Brownlie, collector of Eaton's china; Christine Bourolias, Reference Archivist, Special Collection at the Archives of Ontario: James Bowers, technician at the Archives of Ontario; Mary Rae Shantz, librarian, the Baldwin Room of the Toronto Reference Library; Jodi Aoki, Archives and Special Collections Coordinator at the Bata Library at Trent University, for a new vein of materials about Lady Eaton and Lady Eaton College; Sharon Bentley, librarian at the King City Public Library, for help with Lady Eaton's cookbook collection; Lawrence and Miriam Adams of Dance Collection Danse, for combing the flea market; Pat Phenix, Amy Bowring and Susan Williston at GWL Realty; Ann Cecchia at Oxford University Press. Special thanks to John Denison at Boston Mills Press for believing in this book and to Terrill Maguire for introducing us to ECW Press. Many thanks to Joy Gugeler for editorial magic in a tangled timeline.

Katharine Mallinson would like to thank Janet Zablocki for finding the lost Red Velvet Cake recipe, Joan Caruso for keeping it safe and Zandra Mallinson for helping her bake it.

Carol Anderson would like to thank Michael, Peggy and Eleanor Vaughan.